NOTES FROM EXILE

Notes from Exile

ÉMILE ZOLA

Translated by Dorothy E. Speirs
With 43 photographs by Émile Zola
and a foreword by Captain Glen Vizetelly James
Edited by Dorothy E. Speirs and Yannick Portebois

UNIVERSITY OF TORONTO PRESS
Toronto Buffalo London

© University of Toronto Press Incorporated 2003
Toronto Buffalo London
Printed in Canada

ISBN 0-8020-3747-X (cloth)

Printed on acid-free paper

University of Toronto Romance Series

National Library of Canada Cataloguing in Publication

Zola, Émile, 1840–1902
    Notes from exile / Émile Zola ; translated by Dorothy E. Speirs ;
with 43 photographs by Émile Zola and a foreword by Glen Vizetelly
James ; edited by Dorothy E. Speirs and Yannick Portebois.

(University of Toronto romance series)
Translation of: Pages d'exil.
Includes bibliographical references and index.
ISBN 0-8020-3747-X

1. Zola, Émile, 1840–1902 – Homes and haunts – Surrey. 2. Zola,
Émile, 1840–1902 – Homes and haunts – Surrey – Pictorial works.
3. Novelists, French – 19th century – Biography. I. Speirs, Dorothy E.
II. Portebois, Yannick, 1961– III. Title. IV. Series.

PQ2529.A213 2003   843'.8   C2003-902928-X

University of Toronto Press acknowledges the financial assistance to
its publishing program of the Canada Council for the Arts and the
Ontario Arts Council.

University of Toronto Press acknowledges the financial support for
its publishing activities of the Government of Canada through the
Book Publishing Industry Development Program (BPIDP).

Contents

Foreword

The Vizetelly family were Émile Zola's closest friends in England both before and after the trial by default at Versailles on 18 July 1898, when Zola was sentenced to twelve months' imprisonment on the charge of having libelled Commandant Esterhazy in his famous 'J'Accuse' letter. His particular friend was Ernest Alfred, my grandfather, who, with his family, took care of Zola during his exile in England. In his books, *With Zola in England* and *Emile Zola: Novelist and Reformer*, Ernest gives many details of Zola's stay. He is only one, however, of a quite extraordinary family, and the following is an abridged account of the lives of various members.

The earliest known domicile of the Vizetelly (Vizzetelli) family was the ancient city of Ravenna, which at the time of Augustus Honorius (384–423 A.D.) became the capital of the western Roman Empire. Later, in the Middle Ages, a certain Cesare Vizzetelli was 'Captain of the People' of Ravenna. Subsequently, one or more of the Vizzetelli family fled to Venice after taking part in a conspiracy and started manufacturing glass.

It was as a glass worker that Jacopo James Vizzetelli came to England, either in the last years of the reign of Mary Tudor or in about the first year of that of her sister, Elizabeth I. In any event, the original factory for the making of Venetian glass is supposed to have been established in or about 1557. The date is not certain, but it is known that the factory, which had been established in the old hall of the Crutched Friars in Hart Street, City of London, was destroyed by fire on 4 September 1575.

There was a Henry Vizzetelli buried at the Church of St Botolph, Bishopsgate, in London on 16 October 1691, and it is interesting that one of his descendants, Henry Richard Vizetelly, although born in the parish of St Bride, was baptised in 1820 at St Botolph, Bishopsgate, by Blomfield, Bishop of London. Documents in the Guildhall Library provide evidence that James Vizzetelli, a member of the Stationers' Company, after being elected constable of the united parishes of St Ann, Blackfriars, and St Andrew by the Wardrobe in 1781, altered the spelling of his name to Vizetelly.

It was in or about 1673, during the reign of Charles II, that George Villiers, second duke of Buckingham, established a glassworks at Lambeth, and it was Henry Vizetelly who later became associated with the duke's 'British Cast Plate Glass.'

The Vizetelly family then became printers. James Vizetelly founded a printing business and died in 1760. He had three children, and his son James, by his second marriage in 1775 to Elizabeth Hinde, produced four children, two of whom were twins, James Henry and Mary Mehetabel, born in 1790. It was the marriage of this James to Martha Jane Vaughan in 1816 that produced a family of journalists and war correspondents. The first born, James Thomas George (1818–97) ran a printing and engraving business in the 1850s that specialized in illustrated books. He was joined by the second son, Henry Richard (1820–94), who had served his apprenticeship as a printer, wood engraver, and illustrator. He was the dynamic member of the family and a prolific writer and publisher. He lived in France, the country that features so largely in his writings, for much of his early life. His marriage in 1844 to Ellen Elizabeth, daughter of John Pollard, MD, produced seven children; after her death, he and his second wife, Elizabeth Ansell, had four children. Henry associated with Herbert Ingram, who founded the *London Illustrated News* in 1842, and he subsequently published his own *Pictorial Times* and in 1855 the *Illustrated Times*. During this time Henry and his brother James printed the first English edition of *Uncle Tom's Cabin* and works by Poe and Longfellow.

In 1865 Henry lived in France and Germany as a foreign correspondent and, as an expert wood engraver and artist, was able to illustrate his news items. He was accompanied by his son Edward, at that time a student at the École des Beaux Arts, who became his assistant. Later, Ernest Alfred and his brother Arthur joined the rest of the family in Auteuil and then at Passy. Ernest, Edward, and later Arthur had been at boarding school in Eastbourne. While at Passy, Ernest was placed in a day school called the Institution Nouissel, where he acquired a working knowledge of French and was then coached for the Lycée Bonaparte, where eventually he became a pupil. He was of increasing assistance to his father Henry, who, in spite of his great interest in French literature, was not readily conversant with the language and made a practice of having one of his sons with him; all had their mother's linguistic gifts. In the autumn of 1869 Ernest accompanied his father to Compiègne, where the Imperial Court was resident and, while visiting the chateau on behalf of his father, was presented to Napoleon III, who spoke to him in English, mentioning that he often saw the *Illustrated London News* and the illustrations of French life therein.

Meanwhile, Henry sent his wife, Elizabeth, and children with Edward and Ernest to Saint Servan. Edward then secured an engagement from the *New York Times*, and Ernest was recalled by his father to live with him at a flat at no. 16 Rue de Miromesnil, near the Élysée Palace. For a brief period in the spring of 1869 Henry travelled to Ireland on behalf of the *London Illustrated News* and *Pall Mall Gazette*, and Ernest was left on his own in Paris, although he was frequently visited by his elder brother Edward. With the onset of the Franco-Prussian war in 1870 the lives of Henry and his son Ernest were transformed. On 19 September, when Paris awoke to the sound of gunfire, father and son became war correspondents and would experience the many hardships of the siege that was to follow. Occasionally, a messenger was able to enter Paris, but it was difficult to send news back to England; eventually, Henry used the unpredictable balloon service, photographing his copy and sketches and sending them by successive balloons. There was a restriction on weight, but Ernest arranged for illustrations for the *News* to be handed to the aeronaut, who would post them from wherever he landed. Henry decided to accept the last opportunity afforded to foreigners to leave the city and with his son was reunited with the rest of the family at Saint Servan. Their stay was short lived, and father and son soon resumed reporting on the conflict for the *News*. On his father's return to England, Ernest freelanced and sent reports on the war to his brother in London, who was able to place the copy successfully. When Paris finally fell, Ernest was joined by his father and Edward, and all three reported on every important event of the 'Bloody Week' in the city. Ernest continued reporting on the Continent for several years, and on 25 March 1881 he was the first member of the family since its arrival in England to marry a foreigner, Marie Tissot, daughter of a landowner in Savoy – a family descended from the Tissots of Switzerland. There were four children of the marriage: Violette – a Parisienne by birth – Victor René, my mother Dora Rosalie Louise, and Marie Ernestine.

Ernest finally returned to London in 1886 and embarked on numerous publishing enterprises. At the request of his father Henry, he prepared English versions of Zola's novels but was apprehensive about the reaction of the English public. His father, who had returned in 1880 to revive Vizetelly & Co., was now successfully marketing French novels, selling up to 1000 books per week. By 1888 the firm was selling almost all the novels that Zola had by then written. In 1888, however, the National Vigilance Association attacked Henry for his publications, in particular, *La Terre* (*The Soil*). The House of Commons carried a motion put to the House by Samuel Smith, M.P., 'deploring the rapid spread of demoralising literature.' Meanwhile, Ernest was busy translating and writing on his own account and by this time had formed a close association with Zola.

On 31 October 1888 Henry pleaded guilty in a London court to publishing obscene literature, the English translation of *La Terre*, and was fined £100 and bound over in a further sum of £200 to abstain from repetition of the offence. In spite of this unmistakable warning, Henry decided in 1889 to re-issue Zola's works in a slightly altered form, the work of expurgation being entrusted to his son Ernest. On 30 May 1889 Henry appeared at the Old Bailey, once again charged with publishing obscene literature. He was now in very bad health and was accompanied by Ernest. Alfred Cock, Q.C., was engaged as counsel, and, since they believed the case would last for several days, the Vizetellys voluntarily increased the fee to counsel and assumed the barrister would do his utmost. In the event, Cock withdrew and, after an alleged interview with the solicitor general, persuaded Henry to plead guilty. Thus, the case was never argued on its merits, and the recorder then passed sentence. Henry's recognizances were to be estreated and he must go to prison as a first-class misdemeanant for three months. He spent a considerable part of his detention in the infirmary at Holloway and, in spite of a deputation to the home secretary, was compelled to complete the sentence, being released at the end of August 1889, at the age of sixty-nine. He died on 1 January 1894 after a final, distressing illness and is buried in the small churchyard at Churt, Surrey.

Henry's brother, Francis (1830–83) – always known as Frank – was the youngest of the children of James's first marriage to Martha. He was perhaps the most colourful of the brothers. He founded and for a time edited *Le Monde Illustré* in Paris and subsequently became a war correspondent for the *Illustrated London News*. Frank was sent to cover the war between Sardinia and Austria and then to Sicily to report on Garibaldi's expedition of 1860. He produced abundant and most detailed drawings of the campaign and became a great friend of Garibaldi. In 1861 he was off to America for the *News* to cover the Civil War from both the Union and the Confederate sides. He then moved to St Louis, where he reported on the gunboats on the Mississippi River and made numerous sketches for the *News*. Frank decided to set out for the South and, after a series of adventures, reached Richmond just as the Union army was repulsed at the end of 1862. For almost three years he accompanied the Confederate army, joining them on numerous raids. During this time he sent sketches and portraits to the *News*, but unfortunately some failed to get through the blockade. After witnessing many of the major engagements of the Civil War, Frank sailed for home in 1865 and travelled to Vienna to cover the hostilities between Austria and Prussia. From there he travelled to Spain, Tunis, and Egypt. It was in Egypt that he encountered his nephew Edward during the bombardment of Alexandria in 1882.

Frank arranged to go to the Sudan to join an ill-fated expedition with Hicks Pasha on behalf of the *Graphic* in 1883. The expedition was a disaster. A massacre occurred during an attack by the Mahdi's forces on 3 November 1883. Frank's body was never found. A tablet in memory of the special correspondents who fell in the Sudan was placed in the Crypt of St Paul's Cathedral and records 'Frank Vizetelly, artist, Cashgil, November 1883.'

Henry's elder brother James (1818–97), who died three years after he did, had been one of the mainstays of the family business. The two brothers started a printing and engraving firm known as Vizetelly Brothers, and eventually James established himself under the name of Vizetelly & Co. at 135 Fleet Street, adjacent to the old premises of the company in Peterborough Court. He published several English translations of important French works and later, in conjunction with his younger brother Frank, started a periodical entitled *Echoes of the Clubs*, which was later brought down by a libel suit. A weekly illustrated newspaper, *Passing Events*, went under, owing to insufficient capital. James married Selina Caroline Ward in 1845, a most accomplished woman, who contributed to her husband's work. His brother Henry ran the periodical *The Welcome Guest*, and Selina penned the numerous and highly diverting 'answers to correspondents.' There was one son of the marriage, Montague (1846–97), who had briefly joined his uncle Henry and cousin Ernest in Paris in 1869. He then joined General Chanzy's forces at Le Mans on behalf of the *Daily News*. After the Franco-Prussian war he was sent by the *Times* to cover the Italian campaign in Abysinnia and subsequently to South America by the *Financial Times* and to Newfoundland on behalf of the *Manchester Courier*. He also wrote for the *Daily Chronicle* and *Morning Advertiser* as a specialist on military matters.

Henry's son by his second wife, Frank Horace Vizetelly, Litt D, LLD, was also educated at Eastbourne and in France. He moved to New York in 1891 and became a well-known lexicographer and wrote numerous books on the use of English. He contributed articles to a number of American periodicals and became managing editor of Funk and Wagnalls, New York.

Mention has already been made of Edward Henry Vizetelly (1847–1903), second son of Henry and brother of Ernest and Arthur. He had been at school in Eastbourne with Ernest and then the Lycée de St Omer. He remained in France with his father and in 1870 covered the war in France for the *Daily News* and the *New York Times*. He was another of the family to become a close friend of Garibaldi and was with him in the Vosges; Garibaldi made him one of his 'orderly officers.' In 1871 he covered the uprising in Lyon and in the same year was in Algeria to cover the insurrection. In 1876, tired of Fleet Street and the Strand, he set off for Turkey to participate in the Russia-Turkey quarrel and eventually became a Bashi-Bazouk, or a freelance soldier. Throughout the campaign he sent letters to the *Standard*. From Turkey, he moved to Greece and then to Cyprus, where he founded and edited the *Cyprus Times*. The Arabist movement in Egypt caught his interest, and by the beginning of 1882 he had moved to Cairo, where he represented the *Daily News*. He was also employed on the *Bombay Gazette* and the *Egyptian Gazette*. As hordes of Egyptians were starting to massacre Europeans in Cairo, he fled to Alexandria, where he stayed throughout the bombardment of the city by British warships, a reprisal for the killings in Cairo.

At this juncture Edward was astonished by the arrival of his uncle Frank, just in time for the shelling! A British naval brigade landed, and before long Edward was back in Cairo, where he was later decorated by the Khedive. He met James Gordon Bennett, owner of the *New York Herald*, who persuaded him to use Zanzibar as a base to establish the whereabouts in Africa of Henry M. Stanley, who had been out of touch for eighteen months. He was able to travel through German East Africa only after managing to persuade Prince Otto von Bismarck to give authority, and he organized a column that found Stanley. As promised, Bennett cabled £2000 to Edward's bank. Edward returned to Europe and lived for several years in Paris. Like his brother Ernest, he also married a Frenchwoman, Marie Honorine Clerget. Georgette and Esmé, his youngest daughters, were well known to me until their deaths in recent years. I now own copies of Edward's *Reminiscences of a Bashi-Bazouk* and *From Cyprus to Zanzibar by the Egyptian Delta.*

Sadly, my grandfather Ernest died on 26 March 1922, when I was only three years of age. Apart from his half-brother Frank, who died in New York in 1938, he was the last of an extraordinary family of writers, artists, publishers, and war correspondents. Although I have no memories of my grandfather, I was fortunate to know and love my grand'mère Marie for many years. My brother Clifford and I spent many happy hours at her cottage on Wimbledon Common, which was a focal point for the Vizetellys. My aunt Violette and uncle Victor (daughter and son of Ernest) lived locally, as did Edward Vizetelly's two youngest daughters, Georgette and Esmé. My mother's younger sister, Marie, visited us from Winchester on many occasions. My mother, Dora, was intensely proud of her family, and both my brother and I were christened Vizetelly and my brother's eldest son also bears the name.

Captain Glen Vizetelly James
Beaminster, February 2002

Preface

As we were researching primary material for our forthcoming history of the publishing house of Vizetelly & Co., we were fortunate enough to meet with Captain Glen Vizetelly James and his wife, Mrs Winsome James, and their daughter, Diane James. They generously opened the family archives to us, as well as their very welcoming house in Dorset. The photographs taken by Zola and presented in this book have been in the hands of the Vizetelly family since 1898. They were passed down from generation to generation: from Ernest Vizetelly, Zola's translator and friend, to Dora, Ernest's daughter, to Captain Vizetelly, Dora's son. In reproducing Zola's photographs in this volume, we are including the original captions, which were hand-written on the back of the photographs by Ernest Vizetelly. We wish to thank Dr Robert Jankov, MD (Hospital for Sick Children, Toronto), for his generous technical help and advice in preparing these photographs for publication.

The notes written by Zola while he was in exile in England (18 July 1898 to 5 June 1899) as a result of the Dreyfus Affair had not to date been translated into English. The French text was first published in 1964 by Colin Burns. In his *Pages d'exil*, Zola repeatedly mentions the afternoons he spent cycling in England's countryside, photographing the landscape, which he found lovely. He delighted in what he could see from the window of his house in Surrey: 'the far meadows, bordered with enormous elms and oaks, take on a vaporous lightness, like something from a fairytale.

Perspectives appear, the trees in the distance are only blurred silhouettes. The clumps of trees stand out, delicately coloured. It's the haziness and the quivering of the Elysian Fields, a dream of unending gentleness and melancholy.'

In 2002, on the occasion of the centenary of Zola's tragic death, it seems fitting to offer to the English-reading public these *Notes from Exile*, along with the photographs taken by the novelist. The photographs bring a new dimension to the text, and the reader is able to follow the exiled and rather lonely Zola through small and quiet villages, along the banks of the River Thames, in the fields and the meadows of Surrey ...

D.E.S. & Y.P.
Toronto, October 2002

Chronology of the Dreyfus Affair

1894

20–5 September: The Statistical Section of the Army Intelligence Service, directed by Colonel Jean Sandherr, intercepts a memorandum (the 'bordereau') addressed to Maximilian von Schwartzkoppen, the German military attaché in Paris. At the request of General Auguste Mercier, minister of war, an inquiry is immediately launched in the offices of the general staff.

6 October: Suspicion is cast upon Captain Alfred Dreyfus, a Jewish probationary officer on the general staff.

6–13 October: The 'bordereau' is subjected to a handwriting analysis. When the results of the first analysis are inconclusive, a second analysis is ordered. This second analysis, by Alphonse Bertillon, a fervent anti-Semite, concludes that Dreyfus is the guilty party.

15 October: Dreyfus is arrested and interrogated by Commander Armand Du Paty de Clam, who heads up the investigation. He is incarcerated in the Cherche-Midi prison.

29 October: Two other handwriting experts, Etienne Charavay and Pierre Teyssonnières, confirm Bertillon's analysis.

31 October: Du Paty de Clam submits his report to the War Ministry, but comes to no firm conclusion.

1 November: For the first time, the anti-Semitic newspaper, *La Libre Parole*, mentions Alfred Dreyfus.

3 November: General Félix Saussier, military governor of Paris, orders a judicial investigation of the case and puts Commandant d'Ormescheville in charge.

19 December: Alfred Dreyfus's court martial begins, behind closed doors. He is defended by Edgar Demange.

22 December: Dreyfus is unanimously convicted and sentenced to be deported for life to a prison facility. Before their deliberations began, the judges had illegally obtained a 'secret dossier,' which had been given to them by General Mercier and whose contents laid the blame on Dreyfus.

1895

5 January: Captain Dreyfus is publicly degraded in the main courtyard of the Military College.

17 January: Félix Faure is elected president of the Republic. The same night, Dreyfus leaves France on his way to prison.

7 February: Alfred Dreyfus's brother, Mathieu Dreyfus, contacts Auguste Scheurer-Kestner, vice-president of the Senate, and asks for his assistance in proving the innocence of his brother.

12 March: The boat carrying Alfred Dreyfus arrives in French Guiana.

13 April: Dreyfus arrives on Devil's Island.

1896

1–2 March: The Intelligence Service comes into possession of a telegram written by Schwartzkoppen to Commander Ferdinand Esterhazy. Colonel Georges Picquart decides to investigate Esterhazy and quickly becomes convinced that Esterhazy is the author of the 'bordereau.'

August–September: Picquart informs General Charles Le Mouton de Boisdeffre and General Charles-Arthur Gonse, second-in-command of the general staff, of his suspicions about Esterhazy.

14 September: For the first time, the fact that secret information was given to the war council is revealed in the press.

16 September: Lucie Dreyfus writes to the House, demanding that her husband's case be reviewed.

27 October: General Gonse decides that Picquart must be sent away from Paris: he is sent on a tour of inspection of France's eastern border.

31 October: Colonel Joseph Henry produces a forgery, claiming that it is a correspondence between Alessandro Panizzardi and Schwartzkoppen, the Italian and German military attachés. In the document, Dreyfus is named as the culprit.

6 November: A young Jewish intellectual, Bernard-Lazare, publishes his first pamphlet on the Dreyfus Affair, *Une erreur judiciaire. La vérité sur l'affaire Dreyfus* [*A Judicial Error. The Truth about the Dreyfus Affair*]. In the weeks that follow, he attempts to rally a number of literary and political figures to his cause. Zola is not convinced.

26 December: General Gonse writes to Picquart that his secondment has been extended and that he is to leave for Tunisia.

1897

6 January: General Gonse informs Picquart that he has been temporarily seconded to the Fourth Regiment of Algerian Sharpshooters, based in Sousse, Tunisia.

21–29 June: While on leave in Paris, Picquart tells his lawyer, Louis Leblois, what he has discovered. Convinced that a plot is being hatched against him, he gives Leblois power of attorney over his affairs.

13 July: Leblois tells Scheurer-Kestner what he knows. Although he is bound by secrecy, Scheurer-Kestner decides to mount a campaign to free Dreyfus.

17 August: Esterhazy is relieved of duty because of a 'temporary indisposition.'

10–15 October: General Billot, the war minister, orders that Picquart's mission on the border of Tripoli, where there is unrest, be prolonged.

16 October: General Billot, General Gonse, Colonel Henry, and Commander Du Paty de Clam decide to warn Esterhazy that he is about to become the subject of an inquiry, and two days later Esterhazy receives an anonymous letter to this effect.

23 October: A secret meeting takes place in the Montsouris Park in Paris between Esterhazy and the representatives of the War Ministry (Du Paty de Clam, Henry, and Gribelin). This meeting is followed by a second, a few days later, between Esterhazy and a mysterious 'veiled lady.'

October–November: Scheurer-Kestner begins to lobby actively for an inquiry into the Dreyfus Affair.

5 November: The journalist Gabriel Monod states in *Le Temps* that Dreyfus is the victim of a judicial error.

6 November: Bernard-Lazare visits Zola once again. His second pamphlet, *Une erreur judiciaire. L'affaire Dreyfus*, is about to appear.

11 November: Mathieu Dreyfus learns from Jacques de Castro, a banker, that Esterhazy is the real author of the 'bordereau.' He approaches Scheurer-Kestner with the news, and Scheurer-Kestner confirms the fact.

13 November: A meeting is held at the home of Scheurer-Kestner. Zola attends, along with Leblois, Marcel Prévost, and Louis Sarrut, a lawyer.

15 November: In an open letter published in *Le Temps*, Scheurer-Kestner maintains that Dreyfus is innocent. Schwartzkoppen is recalled by the German government and leaves Paris.

16 November: The morning newspapers publish a letter from Mathieu Dreyfus to the minister of war denouncing Esterhazy as the author of the 'bordereau.'

17 November: As a result of Mathieu Dreyfus's denunciation, an inquiry into Esterhazy's role is launched.

25 November: The first article by Zola appears in *Le Figaro* in support of the Dreyfus cause ('M. Scheurer-Kestner').

1 December: A second article by Zola is published in *Le Figaro* ('Le syndicat').

3 December: Georges-Gabriel de Pellieux reports to General Saussier on his inquiry.

4 December: Another inquiry into the Esterhazy affair is put in the hands of Commander Alexandre-Alfred Ravary. When challenged, President Jules Méline defends himself, saying 'that there is not, nor can there be, any Dreyfus Affair.'

5 December: Another article by Zola appears in *Le Figaro* ('Procès-verbal').

14 December: Zola publishes his 'Lettre à la jeunesse' through the good offices of his publisher, Eugène Fasquelle.

26 December: Three handwriting experts testify in the Ravary inquiry that the handwriting on the 'bordereau' is not Esterhazy's.

1898

1 January: Ravary submits his conclusions: there are no grounds for prosecuting Esterhazy. He will be arraigned nonetheless.

7 January: Another pamphlet by Zola is published: 'Lettre à la France' (Fasquelle). At the same time, Bernand-Lazare publishes his third work, *Comment on condamne un innocent* [*How an innocent man is condemned*].

10 January: Esterhazy's trial begins behind closed doors at the Cherche-Midi prison.

11 January: Esterhazy is acquitted unanimously.

13 January: 'J'Accuse' is published in *L'Aurore.* Albert de Mun challenges the government; Picquart is put under arrest at Mont-Valérien.

14 January: A campaign of protest, signed by a group of 'intellectuals,' begins in *L'Aurore,* demanding that the Dreyfus Affair be reviewed.

18 January: General Billot lodges a complaint against Zola and *L'Aurore.*

19 January: A 'Proletarian demonstration' is begun by the socialist members of Parliament, who rejected involvement in the Dreyfus Affair.

21 January: The three handwriting experts claim that they have been slandered in 'J'Accuse.'

7 February: Zola's trial begins before the Assizes Court of the Seine. Zola makes his statement on 21 February.

23 February: Zola is found guilty of slander and sentenced to the maximum penalty, one year in prison and a 3000 franc fine.

26 February: Picquart is cashiered. Zola lodges an appeal.

5 March: Picquart and Henry fight a duel.

9 March: The three handwriting experts bring a suit against Zola.

2 April: The Criminal Division of the Appeals Court overturns the 23 February judgment against Zola on a technicality.

8 April: A civil suit is brought against Zola by the judges of the tribunal that acquitted Esterhazy.

23 May: Zola's civil trial begins before the court at Versailles.

16 June: Zola's appeal lodged on 26 February is rejected.

18 June: After the fall of the Méline government, Adolphe Brisson takes office and names Godefroy Cavaignac minister of war.

12 July: Both Esterhazy and Picquart are arrested and imprisoned the next day.

18 July: Zola's second trial takes place at the Assizes Court at Versailles. He is found guilty again and, the same evening, leaves for England.

10 August: Jean Jaurès begins a series of pro-Dreyfus articles in *La Petite République.*

13 August: Upon examination of the 'secret dossier,' Captain Louis Cuignet, a member of Cavaignac's staff, discovers Henry's 1896 forgery.

27 August: The commission of inquiry decides to discharge Esterhazy.

30 August: Colonel Henry admits to Cavaignac that he is guilty of the forgery. He is arrested and sent to Mont-Valérien, where he commits suicide the next day.

3 September: Cavaignac resigns.

4 September: Esterhazy leaves France.

26 September: The Council of Ministers declares that they are in favour of a review of the Dreyfus Affair.

8 November: The inquiry begins.

1899

9 February: The inquiry ends.

16 February: Félix Faure, the president of the Republic and a strong adversary of the review, dies. He is replaced by Émile Loubet.

21 March: At the first plenary session of the Court of Appeal Alexis Ballot-Beaupré is designated as chair.

29 March: Ballot-Beaupré presents his report.

1 June: Du Paty de Clam is arrested.

3 June: The verdict of 1894 is overturned and Dreyfus is called before the War Council in Rennes.

5 June: Dreyfus is informed of the verdict. Zola returns to Paris and is finally served with the notice which was issued on 18 July 1898.

9 June: Zola states his opposition to the notice. Picquart leaves prison. Dreyfus leaves Devil's Island on the cruiser *Sfax*.

1 July: Dreyfus arrives in France and is housed in the military prison at Rennes. There, he is given access by his lawyers to the transcripts of Zola's trial (February 1898) and of the deliberations of the Court of Appeal.

7 August: The trial begins at Rennes. An attempt is made on the life of Fernand Labori, Zola's lawyer, on 14 August.

9 September: Dreyfus is once again found guilty, this time with 'extenuating circumstances,' and is sentenced to ten years in prison.

19 September: Dreyfus is pardoned by President Loubet.

17 November: President Waldeck-Rousseau demands an amnesty for all those connected with the Dreyfus Affair.

23 November: Zola's trial is adjourned indefinitely.

1900–8

18 December 1900: The Chamber adopts the amnesty law by a vote of 155 to 2. On 24 December the Senate votes for amnesty by a count of 194 to 10. The law is passed three days later.

29 September 1902: Death of Emile Zola.

26 November 1903: Alfred Dreyfus writes to the minister of justice to demand a review of the Rennes trial. The Rennes verdict is overturned on 12 July 1906.

13 July 1906: The Chamber of Deputies reinstates Dreyfus and Picquart in the army, Dreyfus with the rank of squadron leader and Picquart with that of brigadier.

21 July 1906: Dreyfus receives the Légion d'honneur in the courtyard of the Military Academy.

25 October 1906: Picquart, promoted to major general, becomes minister of war in the first Clemenceau cabinet.

4 June 1908: The official ceremony marking the transfer of Zola's ashes to the Panthéon in Paris takes place. Louis Gregori, a journalist, fires twice at Alfred Dreyfus, wounding him in the arm.

INTRODUCTION

Zola in 1898

His Fame

'I'm surprised,' wrote Zola to a correspondent who complained that Zola hadn't received his letter. 'All you have to do is write 'Émile Zola, France' on an envelope, and the letter will get to me.'[1] This casual remark, in fact, sums up Zola's reputation at the moment he was to leave for exile in England. In 1893 he had completed his monumental twenty-volume novel series, *Les Rougon-Macquart. Histoire naturelle et sociale d'une famille sous le Second Empire*, and in March had just published *Paris*, the third volume of his trilogy, *Les Trois Villes*. For almost twenty years, the publication of a new Zola novel had been an important literary event. The newspaper which obtained the lucrative rights to the serialization would launch an enormous publicity campaign. Edmond Le Roy described the extent to which *Le Journal* went in announcing the forthcoming publication of *Paris*:

> On the streets, at the tram stops, in front of the cafés, at the doors of the department stores, all around the train stations, the passerby stopped, astonished by the flyers, 1.20 meters wide and 80 centimetres high, in colour, depicting some of our most popular novelists. When the flyer was turned over, it read '*Le Journal* is publishing *PARIS* by Émile Zola!' Flyers were also being handed out on the platforms of the buses and the trams, catching the pedestrian's eye, while the passengers already had a flyer in their hands, which they'd been given at the same time as their tickets. At the terminus, supervisors from *Le Journal* handed out more piles of flyers, as more vehicles set out in different directions. You might say that last Friday, from six o'clock in the morning until midnight, everyone in Paris learned, if they didn't know already, that *Paris* was coming out in our *Journal*.[2]

Three days after the end of the serialized publication of the novel, the bookstalls were piled high with the distinctive yellow covers of the Charpentier-Fasquelle edition, and patrons queued impatiently to buy Zola's newest work. Virtually as soon as they appeared, Zola's novels were translated into almost every European language. The novelist himself negotiated all his contracts, without the help of his editor or a literary agent. Generally highly successful, he was nonetheless frustrated on more than one occasion by American 'pirate editions,' which flooded the English-language markets, the United States having refused to sign the 1892 international copyright agreement.

Further, Zola had become a force in the theatre. If his first plays, *Nana, Germinal, Renée,* and *Le Ventre de Paris,* written in collaboration with William Busnach, had been only moderately successful, Zola's partnership with Alfred Bruneau, a talented composer and pupil of Jules Massenet, had opened up new avenues. Writing in collaboration with the dramatist Louis Gallet, Zola saw his 1888 novel, *Le Rêve,* become a stage success, running for an entire season at the Opéra-Comique in Paris. Other libretti were to follow, like *L'Attaque du moulin* in 1893, which played to full houses not only in Paris, but also in Brussels and in London.

Zola, in short, was a high-profile public figure. Every day brought an onslaught of mail: letters from young writers asking him to read their work or to write a preface for a novel or a volume of poetry; letters of admiration for his novels; letters asking for copies of his books, for photographs, for autographs, for help in getting a job, an honorary decoration; letters requesting that he endorse a brand of wine, of cigarettes ... Newpaper editors solicited articles and stories; interviewers by the dozens presented themselves at his Paris apartment and at his country home in Médan. Zola was unfailingly gracious, sharing with them his opinion on matters as diverse as anarchism, cremation, marriage, and whether or not he preferred cats to dogs. Even before the Dreyfus Affair, barely a day went by without Zola's name being mentioned in some context or another on the front page of at least one of the Paris dailies: when his pet dog went missing in 1892, *Le Figaro* carried the announcement on the front page.

His Fortune

The novelist's literary success had ensured his financial stability. Illustrated editions, reprints, newspaper serializations, translations, productions of his plays, all contributed to making a life for Zola and his wife, Alexandrine, that was far more luxurious than the modest existence they had led when they first married in 1870. As Zola's income grew, so did his home in Médan, just outside Paris, with towers and pavilions' being added to receive his numerous guests. However, Zola never coveted money for its own sake. As he told Henri Bryois in an interview for *Le Figaro*: 'When I was young, I knew what real poverty was: I wasn't afraid of it, and I never really envied rich people. I struggled for a long time, and I worked. I made my fortune: I've accepted it, but I spend it freely ... I live a good life and my bookeeper, who is my wife, lets me use my money in order to satisfy my spending whims. I earn a lot, I spend a lot, and I don't know anything about what people call "investing money."'[3]

Decidedly, Zola was a force to be reckoned with in the literary establishment. Honours had come to him: in 1891 he had been elected president of the Société des Gens de Lettres, leading the society's members through debates on censorship, protection of authors' rights, and so forth. He had been nominated knight in 1888, then officer in 1893 of the Légion d'honneur. By 1898 only one honour still eluded him: a seat in the prestigious Académie française. In fact, at the time he left for England, Zola had stood for election to the academy thirteen times in all. Friends were puzzled as to why a man who had opposed everything for which the conservative, right-wing academy stood, should be so persistent in his desire to be admitted. Enemies, of course, put Zola's repeated candidacies down to overweening ambition and an inflated ego. In retrospect, however, it seems clear that his motivation sprang from his desire to see the Naturalist movement acknowledged by the academy and consequently ensured a place in the history of French literature.

His Philosophy

As Zola's professional career had evolved, so, too, had his ideological outlook. Like the *Rougon-Macquart* family saga, the *Three Cities* trilogy presented to the reading public a reflection of current social problems. However, whereas masterpieces like *L'Assommoir* and *Germinal* were characterized by a certain degree of detachment on the part of the novelist, *Lourdes, Rome,* and *Paris* not only highlighted the very real preoccupations of turn-of-the-century French society, like the conflict between science and religion, which was raging on a national scale, they also offered an unambiguous solution: 'Today, many religions are dead, others are dying. More and more, men will rely on science: work will become the universal law ... The man who sets himself a task has a balancing-pole, and can walk without stumbling on the tightrope of life. I don't see him as preoccupied by the hereafter, searching for the key to the universe; he looks at life as a natural phenomenon, one to be lived without explanation.'[4] In many ways, Zola's answers echoed currents which dominated left-wing thought in the 1890s. The equation he makes between science, progress, and happiness may seem naive today, to say the least; for Zola and a number of his contemporaries, however, it was scientific progress, not the Christian dogma of faith, hope, and charity, which held the key to France's future.

Although the *Three Cities* books are not read today as often as are the most celebrated of the *Rougon-Macquart* novels, they were nonetheless extremely popular in their time, selling hundreds of thousands of copies. By 1898, on the eve of his hasty departure for London, Zola's work was well known to the English reading public. Since 1884 Henry Vizetelly and, subsequently, his son Ernest had been publishing English-language translations not only of almost all of Zola's novels, but also of many of his important articles and public declarations. The *Three Cities* had been enthusiastically received in England, lauded not only for the vivid pictures they painted of Lourdes, Rome, and Paris, but also for the messages they contained. The *Daily Graphic,* for example, hailed *Paris,* the third novel in the trilogy, as the work of a rigid moralist.

Zola's Life in England

His Homes

When Zola stepped off the train at Victoria Station on the morning of 19 July 1898, he had in his hand only the address of the hotel that had been recommended to him by his Paris friends. His first letter was to the man who would be his guide, interpreter, and friend during the long months of exile, Ernest Alfred Vizetelly: 'My dear confrère, – Tell nobody in the world, and particularly no newspaper, that I am in London. And oblige me by coming to see me tomorrow, Wednesday, at eleven o'clock, at Grosvenor Hotel. You will ask for M. Pascal. And above all, absolute silence, for the most serious interests are at stake. Cordially, Émile Zola.'[5] Uncertain as to Zola's legal status in England, Vizetelly consulted his own solicitor, F.W. Wareham, who informed him that, since the libel with which Zola had been charged was not covered by the Extradition Act between England and France, Zola was in no direct danger from process servers from across the channel. However, both Vizetelly and Wareham thought it prudent for Zola to keep his whereabouts a secret, in order to escape not only potential attacks from anti-dreyfusard enemies, but also to avoid the hordes of reporters, both French and English, who were already hot on his trail.

Already, on the evening of 19 July, Zola's disappearance had made headlines in the Paris press. Correspondents stated that Zola had left for a tour of Norway. The next day, he was sighted in a train en route for Lucerne, on a bicycle in the Swiss countryside, and arriving in Holland via Brussels. Reports continued unabated, until the anti-dreyfusard *Petit Journal* stated, on 25 July, that all the previous reports had been made in error: Zola was, in fact, still hiding in Paris, waiting for an opportunity to slip out of the country. Fortunately, they continued, the French police were aware of his plans, and were to arrest him immediately if he attempted to flee.

The reality of Zola's presence in London did not long elude the English media. On 26 July the *Morning Leader* announced that Zola was a guest at the Grosvenor Hotel. As a journalist, Vizetelly used his influence with the Press Association to quash the rumours of Zola's arrival in London; but it became apparent that Zola would have to leave the capital. Brighton and Hastings were rejected because of the large foreign tourist population they attracted. After spending a night at the home of F.W. Wareham,

Zola and his friends set out for the calm of the Surrey country-side. Vizetelly recounts with no little satisfaction the subterfuge he invented in order to outwit their pursuers:

> Then the hall porter asked me, 'Where to, sir ?'
>
> 'Charing Cross Station,' I replied, and the next moment we were bowling along Buckingham Palace Road.
>
> Perhaps a minute elapsed before I tapped the cab-roof with my walking stick. On cabby looking down at me, I said, 'Did I tell you Charing Cross just now, driver ? Ah! well, I made a mistake, I meant Waterloo.'
>
> 'Right, sir,' rejoined cabby; and on we went.
>
> It was a paltry device, perhaps, this trick of giving one direction in the hearing of the hotel servants, and then another when the hotel was out of sight. But, as the reader must know, this kind of thing is always done in novels – particularly in detective stories.
>
> And recollections had come to me of some of Gaboriau's tales which long ago I had helped to place before the English public. It might be that the renowned Monsieur Lecoq or his successor, or perchance some English confrère like Mr Sherlock Holmes, would presently be after us, and so it was just as well to play the game according to the orthodox rules of romance. After all, was it not in something akin to a romance that I was living ?[6]

With the help of Wareham and Vizetelly, Zola moved to the outskirts of London, changing residences each time the press got wind of his presence. Weybridge, in Surrey, about twenty-five kilometres from London, was their first choice. From 22 July to 1 August Zola was a guest at the Oatlands Park Hotel, originally built as a country house in 1794 on the site of a hunting lodge on the estate of Henry VIII's Oatlands Palace. According to Ernest Vizetelly, Zola found the park-like setting, at least certain aspects of it, extremely appealing:

> He [was not] particularly impressed by the far-famed grotto which the hotel handbook states 'has no parallel in the world.' The grotto, an artificial affair, the creation of which is due to a Duke of Newcastle,

whom it cost 40,000£, besides giving employment to three men for twenty years, consists of numerous chambers and passages, whose walls are inlaid with coloured spars, shells, coral, ammonites, and crystals. This work is ingenious enough, but when one enters a bathroom and finds a stuffed alligator there, keeping company with a statue of Venus and a terra-cotta of the infant Hercules, one is apt to remember how perilously near the ridiculous is to the sublime.

Ridiculous also to some minds may seem the Duchess of York's dog and monkey cemetery, in which half a hundred of that lady's canine and simian pets lie buried with headstones to their tombs commemorating their virtues. This cemetery, however, greatly commended itself to M. Zola, who, as some may know, is a rare lover of animals.[7]

Here too, however, Zola was soon spotted, this time by a reporter from the *Daily Mail.*

Uncomfortable with his high visibility at the hotel, Zola, with the help of Vizetelly and Fernand Desmoulin, a friend newly arrived from France, next rented a furnished house, 'Penn,' at Oatlands Chase, between Weybridge and Walton-on-Thames. Zola's moving day was not, however, without drama. The day he moved in, Vizetelly wrote to him: 'I hope you're happy with your house. There's only one thing which struck my wife: the number of rosaries she saw in the house. We have to assume the Venables [the owners of the house] are Catholics: we'll have to be very careful.'[8] In spite of Marie Vizetelly's fears (Catholics were viewed at the time as sympathetic to the anti-Dreyfus camp), Zola lived peacefully at 'Penn' from 1 August until 27 August, when the owners of the house returned from holiday.

His next move took him to Spiney Hill in Addlestone, not far from Weybridge, to a house named 'Summerfield.' On 28 August he wrote to his wife, describing his new home:

I moved yesterday, I've taken refuge farther from the capital, in a more deserted spot. The garden is enormous and shady ... Too, the house is more convenient, and the rent is the same. Since I'd only rented the last one for four weeks, and the owner was coming back

from the seaside, I was forced to move. But I was delighted, and I'd
have changed houses anyway, since I no longer felt safe. The prob-
lem was that when I left the hotel, I was foolish enough not to
choose a different name. I rented the house using the same name
that I'd used at the hotel, with the result that when one of the
newspapers reported that I'd stayed at the hotel using the name
that I'd chosen, the owner of the house, when he read the paper,
realized who his tenant was. So I was at his mercy. But I have been
impressed with people's discretion here: the people who have recognized me have all been extremely reserved. Nonetheless, I'm
happier here. I've changed names again, I'm in a spot where no
one will look for me. I'm now absolutely convinced that I can't be
found.[9]

With the onset of fall weather, Zola moved closer to the centre of
London, abandoning his pseudonym 'M. Émile Beauchamp' for
'M. Roger.' He spent a few days (10 to 15 October) at Bailey's
Hotel in Kensington before moving to the Queen's Hotel in
Upper Norwood, not far from the Crystal Palace. He was to
remain at the Queen's Hotel, this time under the name of 'M.
Jean Richard,' until he left once again for France on 4 June 1899.

Daily Life

The *Notes from Exile* make it clear that Zola's daily life in England
was a quiet one. Although he was, to a degree at least, obliged to
live in relative solitude, the situation did not upset him inordi-
nately. Always a rather sedentary individual, Zola quickly settled
into his familiar work routine. There were, furthermore, few
distractions, except for periodic visits from his wife and from
Jeanne (his mistress) and the children.

Unable to speak English, he had only limited contact with those
around him, Vizetelly, his wife, Marie, and their children, Violette
and Victor-René. In August 1898 he wrote to his wife: 'Here I am,
cloistered in a little house, looked after by a maid who doesn't
speak a word of French, and who's supervised by one of Vizetelly's
daughters, who doesn't know much more. Most of the time, I

have to use sign language. I spend entire days without opening
my mouth – I haven't gone out for five days.'[10] By the autumn,
according to Vizetelly, Zola had made some progress with his
English, with a view to 'arriving at a more accurate understanding
of the telegrams from Paris which he found in the London newspapers.'[11] To this end, Vizetelly obtained for Zola a dictionary, a
conversation manual, and an English grammar for French stu-
dents. 'Whenever he felt that he needed a little relaxation,' writes
Vizetelly, 'he took up one or another of these books and read
them, as he put it to me, "from a philosophical point of view."'[12]
By the end of his stay, Zola had assimilated a number of elements
of English grammar and was able to read the 'Dreyfus news' in the
English papers. After a few weeks, Desmoulin arranged for Zola
to receive two Paris newspapers, Le Siècle and L'Aurore, which he
awaited impatiently each day.

The summer of 1898 was particularly hot and humid; however,
Zola's major complaint with English life, as we see in the Notes,
was the food. And if he speaks in his diary of falling back on eggs,
meat, and salad, he confesses to his wife that he has developed a
taste for English jam: 'I eat lots of jam here, it's my fall-back when
I don't like the meals. The jam is extremely good, but they leave
the pits in, which isn't very nice.'[13] Vizetelly, once again, provides
further insights into Zola's tastes:

> As for the cookery to which M. Zola was at certain periods treated,
> he beheld it with wonder and repulsion. His tastes are simple, but
> to him the plain, boiled, watery potato and the equally watery
> greens were abominations. Plum tart, though served hot (why not
> cold, like the French tarte?) might be more or less eatable; but,
> surely, apple pudding – the inveterate breeder of indigestion – was
> the invention of a savage race. And why, when a prime steak was
> grilled, should the cook water it in order to produce 'gravy' instead
> of applying to it a little butter and chopped parsley? ...
> However, a visit to a fishmonger's shop had made him acquainted
> with the haddock, the kipper, and likewise the humble bloater; and
> occasionally, I believe, when his appetite needed a stimulant he
> turned to the smoked fish, which seemed so novel to his palate. The

cook, of course, was mightily incensed thereat. For her part, she most certainly would not eat haddock or kippers for dinner; she had too much self-respect to do such a thing.[14]

Friends and Family

Somewhat depressed, at times, by the weather and often dispirited at the meals produced by his cook, Zola took solace in letters and visits from his friends and family. As far as his correspondence was concerned, Zola relied in large part during the early days of his exile on letters from friends in France and from Vizetelly in England to keep him up to date on the twists and turns of the Dreyfus Affair. Precautions, however, had to be taken. Zola realized that his handwriting might well be recognized and his letters subsequently traced. For this reason, a complicated scheme was devised according to which Zola's letters to France were addressed by Vizetelly and sent to Zola's friend, Doctor Jules Larat, for subsequent distribution. In England, the process was equally complex: 'Proper arrangements had been made with regard to M. Zola's correspondence. His exact whereabouts were kept absolutely secret even from his most intimate friends. Everybody, his wife and Maître Labori also, addressed their letters to Wareham's office in Bishopsgate Street. Here the correspondence was enclosed in a large envelope and redirected to Oatlands.'[15] Fearful, in the early days of his exile, that his mail would be opened by the police, Zola and his friends avoided mentioning Alexandrine Zola, Jeanne Rozerot, and Fernand Desmoulin by name in their letters. Thus, Alexandrine became 'Alex,' Jeanne became 'Jean,' and Fernand Desmoulin became 'Valentin.' Financial arrangements were equally complicated. During Zola's stay in England, money was forwarded by Zola's publisher, Eugène Fasquelle, to Vizetelly's solicitor, F.W. Wareham in England.

The letters written during the exile are extremely revealing of Zola's state of mind at the time. Frustrated by the fact that he was physically removed from the drama of the Dreyfus Affair and, worse, that he was unable even to read about the events in the

newspaper, Zola found solace in his work. Visits from a few intimate friends – 'apart from the Warehams, myself and family, less
than a score of persons,' says Vizetelly,[16] allowed him to keep in
touch with events in France. Zola's French publishers, Georges
Charpentier and Eugène Fasquelle, his English publishers, Andrew Chatto, Percy Spalding, and George P. Brett, and his friends
Fernand Desmoulin, Bernard-Lazare, Yves Guyot, and Théodore
Duret were among the few who breached the novelist's exile.

Visits from Alexandrine, Jeanne, and the children were, in
many ways, far more problematic. In the beginning, Alexandrine
was unable to join her husband, since she was being closely
watched by the French police. Further, in her husband's absence,
she took care of the running of their two homes and many of
Zola's business dealings, among them the projected seizure and
sale of their belongings at the end of September 1898, in order to
cover the costs incurred by the Versailles trial: 'An execution
having been duly levied at his house in the Rue de Bruxelles, a
sale took place there. In the throng which then assembled were
many admirers who hoped to be able to purchase souvenirs. But
Zola had previously arranged that whatever might be the article
first offered for sale, M. Fasquelle, his publisher, should bid the
full amount of the execution. This was done; the auctioneer put
up a Louis XIII table and M. Fasquelle bid thirty-two thousand
francs for it, at which price it became nominally his property.
The sale was then finished, and the would-be buyers of souvenirs
retired disappointed.'[17] When Alexandrine did visit Zola in London, in October and again in December 1898, she fell ill with
a serious case of bronchitis, from which she was very slow to
recover.

Visits from Jeanne and the children, in the summer of 1898 and
the spring of 1899, although a delight to Zola, were equally
fraught with anxieties. On 11 August 1898 they arrived in England for a visit during Denise and Jacques's school break. Immediately, Vizetelly became alarmed: 'If French spies found you here
at "Penn," they'd let it be known that you're in the company of a
lady who is not your wife. ... I fear there would be an enormous
explosion in the press.'[18] Desmoulin echoed Vizetelly's anxieties

from the other side of the Channel: 'If, by bad luck, your hiding place were discovered, don't you think that your *situation*, in the country of "cant," would turn ugly, bringing antipathy and hatred down on your head? ... The protestants, who are in the majority, would turn against you, because of the irregularity of your situation.'[19] Generally compliant, up to this point, with the wishes and instructions of his friends, Zola exploded: 'Thank you for sharing with me your fears about Jeanne and the children's stay here with me. But everything you say, I've already said it to myself, a long time ago. And do you know why I haven't done anything? It's because I don't care! I've had enough, I've had enough, I've had enough! I've done my duty, and I want to be left in peace. ... I've done enough thinking about other people, my friend, and I repeat that I see my public role as finished and I've decided to think only about me and mine. There! I'll take every precaution I can, but I'm not going to become preoccupied by it, because I'm worn out from struggling and from worrying.'[20]

In September 1898, in the midst of all these upsets and all these comings and goings, Zola learned that Pinpin, his favourite dog, had pined away and died. 'I still see him around me,' he wrote to his wife on 28 September. 'He lived at my side for nine years. My suffering is made more intense by the fact that no one understands the suffering. He was really a part of me. Don't ever tell anyone these things, because they'd laugh at me. When I think that I'll never again finish my letter by asking you to pat Monsieur Pin for me! What a dreadful thing, being constantly torn apart from everything we love.'[21]

As upset as if he'd lost a member of the family, Zola began to imagine that his wife, Alexandrine, was gravely ill, but that she was hiding her illness in order not to upset him. Although he was reassured by Jules Larat that all was well, Zola was still recovering in October, when he wrote to Fernand Desmoulin: 'Yes, my old friend, I've been ill, I even had to stay in bed for a while, I was so shaken by recent events. But don't worry, I'm still solid and in reasonably good physical health. It's my heart which is becoming more and more affected – I'm losing my peace of mind.'[22]

His Hobbies: 'La Petite Reine'

In order to restore his peace of mind, Zola took refuge in two of his great loves: his hobbies and his work. Two weeks after his arrival in England, Marie Vizetelly rented a bicycle for Zola, who had been an enthusiastic cyclist since 1893. Nicknamed in France 'la petite reine' (the little queen), the bicycle had become, on both sides of the channel, an extremely popular means of transportation and recreation. In 1890 the 'Touring Club de France' had been founded as a means of popularizing cycling, and in 1892 Zola had been named an honorary member. Special journals, like *Le Vélo* and *Véloce-Sport* had sprung up, and the Touring Club's membership rocketed from 2,500 in 1893 to 110,000 in 1908. Although in his first months as a cyclist Zola had characterized himself as 'very mediocre,'[23] he quickly became more adept. In 1896 he told the journalist Maurice Guillemot that he had become an enthusiast – an 'enragé': 'Every day, after lunch, I get on my bicycle and go to Meulan, or Pontoise ... 40 or 50 kilometres ... I adore it.'[24] In 1895 he had bought a 'vélodromètre' and discovered that the distance separating his Paris apartment from his country house measured 34 kilometres. Zola was unwilling to let his exile get in the way of his passion. As Jeanne and the children prepared to visit him in England, he reminded her to pack their cycling costumes. As is obvious in the *Notes from Exile*, Zola had rather fixed ideas on the appropriate dress for women cyclists.

Zola Photographe

It was during the summer of 1888 that Zola was introduced to photography. Zola and Alexandrine were spending their holiday in Royan in the company of Zola's publisher, Georges Charpentier, and his wife, Fernand Desmoulin, and Alexandrine's cousins, the Labordes. Here, Zola made the acquaintance of Victor Billaud, editor of the *Gazette des bains de mer de Royan* and enthusiastic amateur photographer, who introduced the novelist to what was to become a passion for the rest of his life. Much photographed himself, Zola had become acquainted with a number of Paris's most famous and sought-after photographers – Nadar, Melandri, Carjat, and Pierre Petit. By 1894 Zola had bought a camera and, like most enthusiasts of the time, had learned to develop his own prints in darkrooms he had had built in both his Paris apartment and his house at Médan. As his skills developed, so did his collection of photographic apparatus. In the eight years before his death, Zola took thousands of shots with at least ten different cameras. He experimented with different types of photographic paper and developed a time-delay mechanism that allowed him to pose alongside his subjects. Always fascinated by technology, Zola eagerly tried out new developments in the art: panoramic cameras, celluloid film, new lenses, and the 'box' camera launched by George Eastman in 1888.

In England Zola pursued his craft: 'It was M. Desmoulin who brought the necessary materials – memoranda, cuttings, and a score of scientific works – from Paris ... Desmoulin also brought a hand camera, which likewise proved very acceptable to the master, and enabled him to take many little photographs – almost a complete pictorial record of his English experiences.[25] Unable to develop and print his photographs, Zola sent Vizetelly and Wareham out in search of a shop that would undertake the work for him. Vizetelly's reply is extremely revealing, not only of the prices of the times (when, for example, one of Zola's books in English translation sold for three shillings and sixpence), but also of the habits of English amateur photographers. On 9 September 1898 Vizetelly wrote to Zola:

> Wareham and I checked the prices with several photographers for having your plates developed and fixed and then for having 3 copies of each printed. The prices are much higher than in France. We couldn't find anything like the prices you mentioned. Here's what seems to be the lowest price, assuming the shop is competent and can do a good job: for developing and fixing the plates, 3 shillings a dozen or 28 shillings (22 francs 50 centimes) for 6 dozens. For printing: 1 shilling and sixpence a dozen or 1 franc 90 centimes.

We can't find anything cheaper, except from people whose work doesn't seem acceptable.

In view of these high prices, we haven't done anything yet. This type of undertaking, developing and printing work of amateur photographers, seems very rare here. We went to a dozen shops, here and in London. Several of them refused to do it at any price.[26]

Zola's laconic reply was unambiguous: 'Since I absolutely want the plates developed and proofs printed here, I'm obliged to accept the prices.'[27]

Art critics and historians, when they write about Zola's photographs, are unstinting in their admiration of them. Some praise the originality of Zola's style, the fact that he was unwilling to bow to the habits and clichés of his time: nowhere in his work, for example, do we see the painted backdrops, the benches, the urns, or the potted plants which were ubiquitous in both French and English photography at the time. Others have been struck by how closely Zola's photographs of places and events, like the 1900 Paris World Fair, resemble contemporary photojournalism.[28] Zola was, then, an extremely talented amateur photographer, but he never allowed his passion for photography to interfere with the central focus of his life: his writing.

Nulla Dies Sine Linea

This motto, 'Nulla dies sine linea,'[29] still can be seen, written in letters of gold above the mantelpiece in Zola's study at Médan. It is indisputable that Zola's faith in the healing and stabilizing power of work allowed him to escape, to a certain extent at least, from the worst torments of his exile. As soon as he was settled at 'Penn,' Zola took from the trunk which Desmoulin had delivered his pen, papers, notes, and documentary material, which he would use to compose the first novel of the *Quatre Évangiles* (*Four Gospels*) series, *Fécondité* (*Fruitfulness*). Very quickly, as we see from the *Notes d'Exil*, he took up the same work rhythms for *Fruitfulness* that he had adopted for his twenty-six previous novels: 'Even before the materials for *Fécondité* were brought to him from France he had given an hour or two each day to the penning of notes and impressions for subsequent use. With the arrival of his books and memoranda, work began in a more systematic way. At half-past eight every morning he partook of a cup of coffee and a roll and butter, no more, and shortly after nine he was at his table in a small room overlooking the garden of the house he had rented. And there he remained regularly, hard at work, until the luncheon hour, covering sheet after sheet of quarto paper with serried lines of his firm, characteristic handwriting.'[30] Zola wrote the last line of *Fécondité* on 27 May 1899; in spite of being caught up in the most turbulent period of his life, Zola had managed to complete a 752-page novel as well as a novella, *Angeline*, during the eleven months of his exile.

Exactly a week later, Zola received a cryptic telegram from his wife: 'Cheque postponed. Receipt received. All is well.' This coded message signified to Zola that the courts had granted a review of Dreyfus's conviction and a new court martial. The next day, Zola left England, forever as it would turn out, accompanied by Eugène Fasquelle and his wife, who had come to London to escort him back. Once again, it is Ernest Vizetelly who describes Zola's last evening in London:

> The train started at nine p.m., and we had a full quarter of an hour at our disposal for our leave-takings in the dimly lit station ... There were *au revoirs* and handshakes all round, and messages, too, for one and another ... '*Au revoir, au revoir!*' For another half-minute we could see our dear and illustrious friend at his carriage window waving his arm to us. And then he was gone. The responsibility which had so long rested on Wareham and myself was ended; Émile Zola's exile was virtually over: shortly after five o'clock on the following morning he would once more be in Paris, ready to take his part in the final, crowning act of one of the greatest dramas that the world has ever witnessed. Truth was still marching on, and assuredly nothing would be able to stop it.[31]

The Dreyfus Affair

It is Zola's involvement in the Dreyfus Affair that precipitated his exile in England.[32] This sordid military espionage story, which shook the Third Republic to its foundations, spanned more than ten years, from the first accusations against Captain Alfred Dreyfus in October 1894 to the official rehabilitation of the wrongly accused Dreyfus, in June 1906.[33] It involved the state and the army, several generals and army officials, ministers, journalists, the French courts of justice, and even foreign governments and diplomats – Colonel von Schwartzkoppen and the military attaché Panizzardi from the German and the Italian embassies, respectively. It triggered a new wave of violence and anti-Semitism. France was dramatically polarized and would suffer for several decades from the aftermath of the affair. Above all, the Dreyfus Affair became what is today considered the first truly international 'media event.'

When Zola published 'J'Accuse,' on 13 January 1898 in the socialist newspaper *L'Aurore*, he knew precisely what he was doing. At first incredulous, he had gradually become convinced of the innocence of Captain Dreyfus. He started his campaign on 25 November 1897 with an article supporting the lobby in favour of Dreyfus launched by the vice-president of the French Senate, Auguste Scheurer-Kestner. Zola wrote two other articles, on 1 and 5 December (in *Le Figaro*), and two pamphlets (*Lettre à la jeunesse* and *Lettre à la France*) before publishing 'J'Accuse.' With the first publications, Zola wanted to raise his fellow-countrymen's consciousness. With 'J'Accuse,' he allowed a great number of doubters, who needed more evidence, to voice their concerns: 'The dreyfusard movement as such did not really emerge until after "J'Accuse" and largely as a result of it.'[34]

With this 'open letter' addressed to the president of the French Republic, Félix Faure, Zola went straight to the heart of the matter: he pointed directly at those officials of all ranks who were lying to the French people: General Billot, the war minister; the court martial; Commanders du Paty de Clam and Ravary; Generals Boisdeffre, Gonse, Pellieux, and Mercier; the three handwriting experts, Belhomme, Varinard, and Couard (whose analysis of Dreyfus's writing largely contributed to his being found guilty). As Zola expected, three trials against him followed, initiated by General Billot, the three handwriting experts, and the judges of the court martial. By going to court and fighting openly before the public opinion, Zola, his friends, and supporters of Dreyfus were hoping to force the government to reopen the Dreyfus case. That is the 'connection between the two cases' to which Zola alludes in the first pages of *Notes from Exile*. However, in July 1898 the situation was far from clear. On 18 July Zola appeared before the Versailles court, and it seemed probable that he would be found guilty of slander. In order to avoid being served with legal papers, and to keep the case open, the novelist had to defect, which he did by taking the night train to London.

Why choose England? Although there is little concrete evidence justifying the hasty decision made on 18 July, four reasons can safely be put forth. First, for several decades, if not for at least a century, England had been the 'natural refuge' for French political exiles. One thinks immediately of Louis-Philippe d'Orléans and his family, forced to leave France after the fall of the monarchy in February 1848; of the leaders of the Republic of 1848, and of Victor Hugo, forced to leave France for the Channel Islands after Napoléon III's coup in December 1851; of the imperial family, forced to leave France after September 1870; of the leaders of the Paris Commune, forced to leave France after May 1871. One could go on and find examples throughout the history of France, up to the Second World War, when General de Gaulle took refuge in London. Thus, England seemed a safe haven for Zola.

The second reason was undoubtedly the fact that the British people were, generally speaking, in favour of Dreyfus. In the days following the publication of 'J'Accuse,' several British newspapers had published articles and comments on the French situation. The *Times*, the *Daily Telegraph*, and the *Manchester Guardian* were 'troubled' by Zola's allegations.[35] Throughout the affair and until the end of 1899 the British press supported Zola's demands for justice. Ernest Vizetelly himself contributed several articles to the *Westminster Gazette*, although he used only parsimoniously the wealth of information he had at his disposal, being on the front line.[36] He also translated the pamphlets written by Zola, thus furthering the Dreyfus cause with the public. The public seemed to share the views of the press; on 11 September 1899, after

Dreyfus's second trial, a huge protest was organized in Hyde Park. Over 80,000 people gathered and demanded Dreyfus's immediate release from prison. Futher, Zola was well loved in England. When he visited London in 1893 as guest speaker during the congress of the Institute of Journalists, Zola had been welcomed 'like royalty,' as he himself stated.[37] The sad days of the pornography trials (in 1888 and 1889)[38] were long gone, and Zola was now perceived as the champion of freedom and justice. Last, but not least, Zola had a staunch supporter and admirer in England: Ernest Vizetelly.

NOTES

1 Zola, *Correspondance*, vol. IV, letter 383; henceforth cited *CZ*.
2 'À propos d'un nouveau roman.'
3 'Les trois derniers livres des *Rougon-Macquart*.'
4 Interview given to Henry Spont, 'L'évolution sociale et la jeunesse.'
5 Vizetelly, *With Zola in England*, 16–17. On Zola's involvement in the Dreyfus Affair, the reason for his coming to England, see the section on the Dreyfus Affair, below, pp. 18–20.
6 Vizetelly, *With Zola in England*, 44–5.
7 Ibid., 74–5.
8 Speirs and Portebois, '*Mon cher Maître*,' 227.
9 Zola, *Correspondance*, vol. IX, letter 185.
10 Ibid., letter 166.
11 Vizetelly, *With Zola in England*, 145.
12 Ibid.
13 Zola, *Correspondance*, vol. IX, letter 201.
14 Vizetelly, *With Zola in England*, 130–1.
15 Ibid., 85.
16 Ibid., 196.
17 Vizetelly, *Émile Zola*, 476.
18 Speirs and Portebois, '*Mon cher Maître*,' 231.
19 Letter of 11 August 1898 (B.N., MSS, n.a.f. 24517, fols 486–7). It should be noted that the British were predominantly pro-Dreyfus. See the next section on the Dreyfus Affair.

20 Zola, *Correspondance*, vol. IX, letter 173. Zola, of course, never
    mentioned Jeanne or the children in the *Notes d'Exil*, since he
    realized that Alexandrine would almost surely read this journal.

21 Ibid., letter 213.

22 Ibid., letter 220.

23 Ibid., vol. X, letter 422.

24 Guillemot, *Villégiatures d'artistes*, 96.

25 Vizetelly, *With Zola in England*, 84.

26 Speirs and Portebois, 'Mon cher Maître,' 238–9.

27 Zola, *Correspondance*, vol. IX, letter 198.

28 See Massin, 'Émile Zola'; Cohenoff, 'Zola et la photographie.'

29 'Never a day without a line.'

30 Vizetelly, *With Zola in England*, 119–20.

31 Ibid., 217–18.

32 The reader will find a brief chronology of the main events of the
    Affair above, pp. xvii–xxv. A very detailed chronology was prepared
    by Alain Pagès and Owen Morgan and published in volume IX of
    the *Correspondance* of Zola (50–62). See also, in the bibliography, the
    works of Kleeblatt, Pagès, and Wilson.

33 In October 1894 Dreyfus was accused, and found guilty after a
    botched trial, of selling military secrets to the Germans. He was sent
    to Devil's Island in January 1895, where he stayed until July 1899.

34 'Zola and the Dreyfus Affair,' Wilson, 3.

35 See Burns, 'Le retentissement de l'Affaire Dreyfus.'

36 Speirs and Portebois, 'Emile Zola in the *Westminster Gazette*.'

37 See Burns, 'Le voyage de Zola à Londres en 1893'; also n. 2 of the
    Notes from Exile, below.

38 See the introduction of Speirs and Portebois, '*Mon cher Maître*,' for
    more details about both trials.

NOTES FROM EXILE

Monday, 18 July 1898.[1] Desmoulin and I leave the Rue de Bruxelles at eight o'clock in the morning. (I wasn't to return: we were so confident that the appeal would defer further enquiries regarding the connection between the two cases[2] that nothing was ready for my departure that evening, since the departure was completely unexpected. I didn't say goodbye to anyone at home, didn't even hug Pinpin.) We ate breakfast at the Charpentier's, where Jane[3] welcomed us. Left in a carriage at a quarter to ten. Through the Bois de Boulogne and Sèvres. Arrived at Versailles about eleven twenty. As soon as we left Viroflay, police on bicycles came to meet us. Police all along the Avenue de Paris, officers every fifty feet.[4] Not many people in the streets, a few shouts when we arrived at the courtroom. The court session. Some said that the atmosphere had changed – the army representatives appeared calm, but worried; at the time, I wasn't aware of it. We, on the other hand, were shouted at when we rose to present our appeal. Then, when we left for the day, my anxiety: it appeared as if we were running away. Perrenx didn't even come back into the courtroom after he had testified. They whisked him away. We went straight to the office which they had set aside for us. Labori, Clemenceau, and the others all advised me to leave France, so that I couldn't be served with the court's decision. The arguments and the unanimity of the group, Labori's fear that if the decision came down right away, I could be served notice immediately, right in the office, before we had the opportunity to leave. M. Mouquin, the chief of police, asked us to wait half an hour so that he could organize his men and allow us to leave quietly. Our anxiety and our impatience. Finally, M. Mouquin came and told us that the carriage was there, and that we could leave. We were to take the Avenue de Paris, then, at the end of the avenue, turn and go up the hill and leave through Garches. This went extremely well. Labori came with me in the carriage, and two fine horses took us away. As we were leaving the courthouse and turning onto the Avenue de Paris, we were spotted by the crowd. The cavalry charged the screaming mob. Mounted officers rode along with us for a bit. Then, all along the avenue, from both sides, all we heard were distant cries. A few groups charged towards us, but they were pushed back. Lines of police stayed behind us and stopped the crowds. And it was in this way that we managed to get away and turn into the small road which led to Garches. At that point, even the police on bicycles had left us, and we continued our trip in complete solitude and silence. Not a soul in the silent forest. It must have been about three thirty in the afternoon, and we were dying of hunger. That morning, I'd taken a bit of bread with me, and I shared it with Labori. As we spoke, we kept coming back to the fact that I must leave immediately if I wanted to play my cards right. I had already decided to leave, in fact, but my heart was heavy. We returned via Saint-Cloud and came back to Charpentier's house through the Bois de Boulogne. We invited the Clemenceaus to come for a last meeting. They arrived with Desmoulin. After we talked, we decided that the best plan would be for me to leave for London that very night, at nine o'clock. But my wife didn't even know – I hadn't seen her since that morning. Desmoulin went to warn her. She arrived, very upset, not even having dared to pack a bag for me, bringing only a nightshirt and a few other things wrapped in a newspaper. And this is all the baggage I had when the two of us arrived by carriage at the Gare du Nord. We were overwhelmed by the suddenness of my departure. I held her hand and squeezed it hard: we spoke only a few words to each other. Charpentier, who had followed in another carriage, bought a ticket to London for me, and he and my wife came with me to the train, where they stayed for fifteen minutes, waiting for the train to leave, shielding the window of the coach, which was the first one behind the engine. What a wrenching separation! My dear wife watched me leave, with her eyes full of tears and her hands clasped and trembling.

All the way to Calais I was alone in the compartment. Since that morning, I had hardly had time to think. My chest was tight with anxiety, and my hands and face felt as if they were on fire. I opened the train window and pulled the shade on the lamp; in the darkness, with a cool breeze coming in, I was finally able to calm down, to cool off, and to think a bit. And what thoughts! To think that, after a lifetime of work, I would be forced to leave Paris, the city which I've loved and celebrated in my writings, in such a way! I hadn't been able to eat at Charpentier's. The day had left such a bitter taste in my mouth that even a piece of bread would have choked me. Now that I was a bit calmer, I was ravenously hungry, and, luckily, at Amiens I was able to buy a roll and a chicken leg. After that, all the way to Calais, I remained wrapped in my thoughts. I admit that they weren't particularly happy: my heart was overflowing with sadness and anger.

Finally, I found myself on the boat, leaving the dock. That was that: I was no longer in France. I looked at my watch: it was half past one in the morning. The sky was clear, although there was no moon, and it was very dark. There couldn't have been more than thirty passengers on the boat, all of them English. And I stayed on the deck, watching the lights of Calais wink out in the darkness. I confess that my eyes filled with tears and that I had never in my life experienced such deep unhappiness. Of course I didn't expect to be leaving my homeland for ever – I knew that I would be back in a few months, that my leaving was only a tactical move. But nonetheless, what a terrible situation – to have striven only for truth and justice, to have dreamed only of preserving in the eyes of her neighbours the good name of a generous and free France – and to find myself forced to flee like this, with only a nightshirt wrapped in a newspaper! Too, certain vile newspapers had poisoned and misled France so completely that I could still hear people shouting at me, me, a man who had always worked for the glory of France and who had only wanted to be the defender who would show France's true greatness among other nations. And to think that I had to leave like this, all alone, without a friend by my side, without anyone to whom I could talk about the horrible rancour which was choking me. I have already suffered a great deal in my life, but I have never undergone a more terrible experience than this one.

The wind became very high, and I hadn't brought an overcoat. Nevertheless, I stayed on the deck, where the brisk, cool wind calmed me. The sea was hardly moving. During the short crossing, thin clouds covered the sky. The clouds lightened as the dawn broke. When I arrived in Dover, day was breaking, and the gas lamps in the small port town paled as the skies brightened. I don't know a word of English, and here I am in a foreign world, as if I were separated from mankind. I hate travelling. I am sedentary almost to the point of phobia, only happy in my own familiar surroundings. I don't like being abroad, I feel horribly homesick, disoriented by all these new things which I don't understand and which upset me. The first few hours of my stay in any country whatsoever outside France are especially trying for me: I experience a feeling of revolt, of distress at understanding nothing. It's curious that, when my enemies insult me, they call me 'the foreigner.' Oh God! how foolish these people are and how little they understand what they're saying! So here I am in Dover, where I can't even ask for a glass of milk. I take refuge in a compartment of the train which will take me to Victoria Station. And I wait there. Half an hour, three-quarters of an hour pass, a horrible wait! I don't know the reason for the delay. The dull day clears up, and, on the dock, the workers pass, dragging their feet. And not another sound – I feel as if I am alone in the train. An overwhelming feeling of being abandoned. Finally, the train leaves, and I doze during the trip, overcome by a crushing fatigue. It's almost eight o'clock when I arrive in London. It's pouring rain; the city seems to be still asleep in a ghastly fog. Paris was so warm and sunny when I left. I remember my short trip to London four years ago, when I was invited by the English press with a group of other French journalists.[5] What a splendid, brotherly welcome we received – a reception and speeches at the station, a party put on by the lord mayor, a gala at Covent Garden, a banquet at the Crystal Palace, not to mention all the private lunch- and dinner-parties. And here I am, getting off the train alone at Victoria, with my nightshirt in a newspaper and walking in the rain to the nearby Grosvenor Hotel,[6] where I have to wait for a quarter of an hour before they find a waiter who can speak French. In the huge entrance hall, a group of English chambermaids, clean and attractive in their bright uniforms, were cleaning the white tiles with sawdust, all on their knees like busy blonde ants. The fact that I have no bags whatsoever embarrassed me. They checked me in anyway, taking a pound for a deposit and telling me that this is what they do for people who arrive without luggage. I registered under the name of M. Pascal, from Paris, and was given a room on the fifth floor, whose window was blocked by the fretwork frieze which adorns the huge building: a foretaste of prison. What an odd building this hotel is, a huge rectangle whose decorations are so bizarre that there isn't a single window that looks like a window. The air and light vents in the rooms, especially on the top floors, look like basement windows, or port-holes, or fanlights in a closet! Nonetheless, I was relieved to be there and to be able to clean up a bit and rest in the calm I felt around me. No one in the world knew I was there, except for a few good friends whom I had told before I left which hotel I was going to. What a change that would be from Paris, where for the last five months, I couldn't move without being recognized and insulted. A first day of confused drowsiness. I had to buy a few things to wear and some odds and ends. God knows the trouble I had making myself understood in the stores! As we'd arranged, I sent my wife a telegram to reassure her, and I wrote a few letters to friends, taking the precautionary measures we'd agreed upon.[7]

Tuesday 19 July. Arrival in London. Grosvenor Hotel. Telegram to my wife. Letter. Rest. After lunch, shopping. I sit in the garden (Grosvenor). Bed at midnight after the article. I'll take a bath in the morning. Meeting with Vizetelly.[8]

Wednesday 20 July. At seven o'clock, Desmoulin knocks and wakes me. M. Pascal. Desmoulin has come with B[ernard] L[azare].[9] They're asking me for an article for *L'Aurore*.[10] In fact I'd done it the day before in anticipation. I give two powers of attorney on legal paper. News from Paris about my 'flight.' Vizetelly, who was to come at eleven o'clock, doesn't arrive until half-past twelve. We were going out to eat at a restaurant, when I was recognized by two women (the wife of Chatto's partner).[11] We go back to eat at the hotel, B.L. leaves for France at two thirty. Desmoulin accom-panies him to Charing Cross, then goes to see if M. Moulton, a lawyer and a friend of Labori, is in London. He's out of town, looking for a government seat. I waited for Desmoulin with Vizetelly, who's going to put me in touch with M. Wareham, a solicitor. We go and sit down in the garden, near a fountain. Children. (The streets of London.) We go on foot to Westminster Bridge. We return to the hotel and I sleep in a different room.

Thursday 21 July. We wait for Vizetelly who is to take me to see Wareham. I spend the morning in my room. Vizetelly arrives as Desmoulin is leaving. Wareham won't be back until two o'clock. We're going to have lunch out, across from Victoria Station. At two o'clock, Wareham arrives. Meeting in the billiard room of the hotel. Can they serve notice on me? I'm too likely to be recognized at the Grosvenor Hotel, so Wareham offers me a room for the night. For the next several days, Vizetelly will pick up any letters for M. Pascal from the hotel. At five o'clock, we take the train from Waterloo Station to Wimbledon. We have dinner in a restaurant. And I spend the night at Wareham's home, while Desmoulin spends the night in another house with the solicitor's clerk. When Desmoulin and Vizetelly leave, I spend the evening with the solicitor and his wife, who don't speak a word of French.

Friday 22 July. Vizetelly is here at nine thirty. The whole morning in a carriage, looking for a furnished house to rent. Wimbledon Common. Walking. Houses we've already looked at. I'm not sure – I don't want to rent anything yet. We have lunch at the Italian restaurant where we ate yesterday (it seems that he recognizes me). And, at two thirty, we decide to leave for Oatlands Park Hotel in Weybridge. We get off at the Walton station. Chilly reception at the hotel. At last, we're given rooms, but only until Sunday night. That night, Vizetelly and Wareham are to come to visit us. Vizetelly leaves us. Desmoulin and I are alone. The hotel and its park, a splendid setting. That evening, we buy shirts, we go for a walk down the road. The holly hedges in the shadows. It has rained, the road is muddy. Only Fritz, a German, speaks French.

Saturday 23 July. The whole morning in our rooms. I can finally take a bath. After lunch at one o'clock, we go for a long walk to Weybridge and the Thames. A rest for a moment on the grass, two

The road to Walton, from Oatlands Park

fine dogs in a boat. Then up to the station, where we get a
carriage to bring us back to the hotel, where we find the rental
agent, Waterer, who gives us four addresses. Then we take a
carriage to visit the houses: we have to come back if we wish to see
the first one, the second is already rented, we don't like the third,
and we then arrive at 'Penn,' a charming house surrounded by
trees. Five guineas a week. We promise to return the next day with
Vizetelly. Back to the hotel. Desmoulin, who is desperate for news,
can find only what's in the English papers. I prefer to know
nothing (what's the psychology behind that?) In any case, no one
knows where I am. The hypotheses in the Paris papers amuse us.[12]
Make the best of this situation as voluntary exiles, cut off from the
news. Our evening on a bench, looking over the fields through
which the Thames flows. Two magnificent elm trees, the bench.
The whole park and the hotel.

The Thames, near Walton 1

Sunday 24 July. A gorgeous day, wonderfully mild, with clear, bright sunshine. The only really nice day so far. After breakfast at nine o'clock, we took a walk past 'Penn.' The countryside is really magnificent, with this sunshine. Describe it. Vizetelly, Wareham, and their wives arrive at three o'clock. The previous evening, sitting on the bench, and again this morning, we decided that Desmoulin should leave this evening for Paris. He'll go and organize things with my wife. He'll be more useful there than here. The emotions we felt, yesterday evening on the bench, with everything we said to each other. Vizetelly and Wareham bring some French newspapers for Desmoulin, who devours them: still nothing, they know nothing. While Desmoulin goes up to write letters in my room, I go to see 'Penn' with the Vizetellys and the Warehams. The house, the lady who serves us tea. We agree that we'll give our final answer by Wednesday. A gorgeous sunset,

The Thames, near Walton 2

dinner at the hotel, the Louis XVI windows. Then, the departure. Deeply touched, Desmoulin and I embrace. He takes my letters and my instructions. He will sleep at Charing Cross tonight and will be in Paris tomorrow at six o'clock in the morning. I'm alone, I go to bed.

Monday 25 July. Very mild day. Silence is the best medicine. I find being alone infinitely calming. Vizetelly sent me some books, among them *Le Rouge et le noir* and *La Chartreuse de Parme.*[13] I spend the morning in my room, writing a note for Labori. Then I spend the afternoon in the park, reading *La Chartreuse de Parme.* I know I won't receive any news today, and that calms me enormously. I can't speak to anyone. During meals, I exchange only a few necessary words with Fritz. Very pleasant evening sitting on my bench, under the giant elm tree.

Tuesday 26 July. Another good morning. Up at nine o'clock. I stay in my room and begin writing up these notes. But right after lunch, at one o'clock, my peace is shattered. Vizetelly has sent me newspapers which report on what is happening at Médan and Verneuil.[14] What wretches to follow women and terrorize them! I also receive letters, one from Labori and one from my wife, full of sadness and anxiety. I'm right back in all the horrors. (Across from me, the wide lawn where English ladies and gentlemen play games, sometimes applauding.) While I'm up in my room answering Labori with a long letter, Mrs Vizetelly arrives, bringing a letter which she thought was for me (it was for Desmoulin), and she tells me that the London papers are saying that I've been seen here in London.[15] This is too much: I'll have to move again, hide again. I'll wait for dinnertime in the park, my thoughts: why continue to hide, why not choose a spot, have my wife join me and wait for things to happen? If they do serve notice on me, and if the notice is deemed valid, I could always go back and give myself up, proclaiming that they want to suppress the truth. And if it's not valid, the trial will begin again, our tactics will have won the day. I've had enough. I spend the evening thinking, wondering where and how I'll live. That combined with reading *La Chartreuse de Parme.*[16] The whole psychology of this day, in the park, with the back-and-forth of my decisions and intervals of reading.

Wednesday 27 July. Peaceful day, I read and I write letters. *La Chartreuse de Parme.* All the thoughts coming out of what I read. Fabrice's situation and mine; integrate that into my impressions. A storm during the day; no thunder, but a torrential rain for more than an hour. Since I don't have an umbrella, I don't venture out of the hotel park. My walks on the terrace with the Thames in the distance, the woody paths in the park. My most worrisome moments are those when I am in the main dining room, where I might be recognized. I'm told that my picture is in a number of shop windows in London. But one good thing about the English is that they don't pay attention to anyone. Everyone here is upper middle class: bourgeois and merchants. The hotel is expensive. The manager, who welcomed Desmoulin and me so coldly, has warmed up. He's realized that we're decent people after all, even though we arrived without suitcases. He has a little white dog which he and his wife seem to adore; they let it run all through the house and the garden, without a muzzle, although up until now I haven't seen a single dog on English soil without a muzzle. They, too, must be decent people. I had to change rooms. They've put me on the third floor, in the tower. The room is enormous, but it has only two chairs, no armchair, which isn't very comfortable for reading. Fortunately, the view is wonderful from the two windows. I'm writing these notes looking out on a magnificent landscape. I was expecting Vizetelly and Wareham at six o'clock, but they didn't arrive until seven, when I was sitting down to dinner. After dinner, we went up to my room for a meeting, and I decided that I will rent the little house called 'Penn.' They left to settle things with the owner on the way back to the station. I read a few pages of *La Chartreuse de Parme*, then went to bed. Wareham had brought me a few letters from France. My wife still can't come to join me, but things seem to be going fairly well.

Thursday 28 July. Very peaceful day. No one came. Still no newspapers. I don't know what is happening, and I am delighted. It rains on and off, I don't dare to go far, I stay in my room, I go for short walks in the park. There, in the afternoon, I'm taken by surprise by a heavy shower, and I take shelter in a rustic cabin made from tree trunks. I spend a delightful hour there, completely alone, with the rain outside, reading *La Chartreuse de Parme*. It's an extraordinary book, and I have the feeling that I'm reading it for the first time. I must not have read it carefully before.[17] It awakens in me a world of admiration and of objections. In the morning, there's a telegram from Wareham, informing me that he had received the money I was expecting,[18] which pleased me; for I discover that a great deal of the anxiety I was feeling came from the fact that I was almost without money and at the mercy of events. In the evening, a letter from Vizetelly, telling me that I cannot take occupancy of the house until Monday, 1 August, which annoys me greatly. Three more days here – might I not be recognized? I'm fascinated by the double-hung windows used almost exclusively in the building. Why do they make them like this? They seem to me so awkward – I'm not used to them. Is it so that they won't rattle when the wind is high? To keep out the cold better and to protect better from the winter and the fog? None of these reasons, which don't concern me anyway, explains why these windows are thought to be superior. As far as I'm concerned, they're like prison windows, windows one can never open completely and at which one can't lean comfortably as one can in front of our French windows![19] The game on the lawn, cricket, I think, continues to puzzle me as well.

Friday 29 July. This morning around eleven o'clock, just as I had written to him, my friend Desmoulin arrived from France. I didn't expect him so soon. Finally, he brings me a trunk of clothing and personal effects, and I experience an enormous pleasure at seeing these intimate objects which bring a bit of my home with them. I'm sure that what troubles me the most about my hasty departure, besides being brutally torn away from those I love, is finding myself far from home with only the clothes on my back, with no baggage and almost no money. My friend Desmoulin brings me news of my wife, my loved ones, and my friends. Things don't seem to be going too badly, but my wife still feels that she can't join me yet. Desmoulin is extremely optimistic, although I don't think that this terrible crisis will be over in the near future. We have lunch, then we take a walk to Walton, which is twenty-five minutes away. And as we walk, I explain my ideas to him: the fact that it is impossible that we could be victorious so soon, without a revolution; and I tell him my plan – to stop hiding and to wait, in order to return when victory is imminent. God knows when! All this would have to be thought out. The news he brings me from Paris which seems to indicate a mounting fever, an ever-faster movement towards the truth. Walton is a lovely little town. I buy an umbrella there. We walk down to the edge of the Thames, and, thinking that we were going into a hotel, we enter into a strange place,[20] where we see the most bizarre sight in the world: a tall girl serves us, a big girl about sixteen or seventeen years old, wearing

The Thames, near Walton 3

a short dress like a baby, a white dress without a belt, which makes her look like a sort of giant child. White stockings, white shoes, she's dressed all in white. And two enormous tufts of curly brown hair, a vaguely Assyrian hairdo. She looked like a girl at her first communion, or one of those Baroque virgins painted by our symbolist aesthetes. Her face was very dirty. In the next room, I glimpsed a miniature of this extraordinary girl, another one, smaller, ten or twelve years old, but absolutely the same. I'd like to know where we actually were. When we got back to the hotel, Desmoulin went to have a rest. While he did, I had a visit with Vizetelly, who came to have me sign the lease for the rental of the house. Everything is fine. I take possession on the first of August. I told Vizetelly that he and Wareham should be careful of the police, since I'm afraid that the French police had opened some of my letters in which I'd given Wareham's address, as my intermediary.

The village of Walton

Before going to bed, I finished reading *La Chartreuse de Parme*. I must note the ideas that I had while reading the work.

Saturday 30 July. The sun reappeared today. I hadn't seen it since Sunday. I continued writing these notes in the morning, before leaving my room. Desmoulin joined me at eleven thirty. I persuaded him to go to London to ask Wareham to rent a bicycle for me and to buy some photographic plates, so that we could take some pictures of the hotel and the park with the lens that my wife had put in the trunk.[21] He left at noon and didn't get back until eight thirty at night, which worried me a great deal, since I was expecting him at five o'clock and I was afraid he'd had an accident. All the more so, since Wareham arrived just before seven o'clock and told me that he hadn't seen him. Wareham had come to ask me if he could give my address to someone who had given

The church of Walton

him Labori's card.[22] He had refused outright to say anything without having asked me first. I appreciate his discretion. This message from Labori, which I won't know about until tomorrow, depressed me. It seems clear that I'm not to be left alone, I'm not to be allowed to forget what's going on and to get back to work. When the errant Desmoulin got back, he explained that he'd arrived at Wareham's after Wareham had left and that he'd then got on the wrong train. Oh well, he's not hurt, everything's fine. He brought me some photographic plates. During the day, I began to read Balzac's *L'Envers de l'histoire contemporaine.*

Sunday 31 July. Another splendid day, with bright and warm sunshine. When the sky is blue, the countryside is superb, with its deep, enormous woods, always cool. In the morning, when Desmoulin had come to my room and we were getting ready to take some photographs in the hotel park, Vizetelly arrived. He and Wareham were uneasy and decided not to give my address to the person sent by Labori. This overzealousness, which is going to complicate matters, does not displease me nonetheless. Labori sends me two issues of *La Petite République française,* in which there are very detailed articles that seem to prove that Colonel Combe's letters against my father, which were published in *Le Petit Journal,* are forgeries, or at least have been falsified.[23] He asks me to send him the indictment I had sent to the public prosecutor, in which I accuse the author of forgery. We decide that Desmoulin will go to London to deal with the envoy; at six o'clock that evening, he returns with Labori's letter and the outline of the indictment. I immediately copied the draft onto a sheet of official foolscap, so that tomorrow Desmoulin can return to London to give the form back to the envoy, who will be back in Paris tomorrow evening. How complicated it all is! All the more so, since today is Sunday and tomorrow is a holiday (bank holiday). Everything is shut, the trains hardly run, you can't imagine the difficulty we had laying hands on a sheet of official foolscap. So I spent the whole day alone. Towards noon, I took a few photographs which I want to take with me. I continued reading *L'Envers de l'histoire contemporaine.* It's a very odd book, and it disgusts me a bit, since it represents the opposite of all my literary and social beliefs. But most of all I thought about what is going on in Paris, as I read the two issues of *La Petite République* I had been sent. There's no sense to any of it.

Monday, 1 August. At last, today, I left the hotel and moved into the little house called 'Penn.' The precise address is: 'Penn,' Oatlands Chase, Weybridge, Surrey. Wareham rented it for four weeks in the name of M. Jean Beauchamp, and everything is fine. I'm home, I can breathe. I stayed for ten whole days at the Oatlands Park Hotel, and it's a miracle that no one recognized me, because the turnover of travellers is a lot higher there than I would have thought. Every day there were between sixty and eighty people in the large dining room, and the faces changed often. This morning, Desmoulin went back to London to give the indictment to Labori's envoy. He won't be back to pick me up until three o'clock. I spent the day reading; I began *Le Rouge et le noir.*[24] I went to say goodbye to the park with the magnificent trees and, as I usually do when I leave a place where I've stayed for a while, even when I've been troubled, I was a bit emotional. At three o'clock, we left from the station with our bags, so that it would appear as if we were leaving the country. We told the hotel manager that since Mme Beauchamp still could not join us, we were returning to London, but that we would undoubtedly return with Mme Beauchamp as soon as she got to England. At the station, we were met by Wareham, Mme Vizetelly, her daughter, Violette, and the maid, Louise. Louise can't speak a word of French, but Violette, who speaks it well, is going to stay with me to act as my interpreter. So we returned to 'Penn' with our baggage and moved in. Mme Vizetelly had brought me a whole basket of shopping — groceries, butter, and a roast chicken for tonight. I settled up with her and with Wareham, who gave me the money which Fasquelle had sent. We made up the beds, and then we were left alone, Desmoulin and I, with Violette and Louise. After dinner, our first evening was very pleasant in this quiet little house. The evening was superb, a magnificent moon. We stayed in the living room until half-past nine, talking affectionately among ourselves, still a bit surprised to be there. This little house, with its bright paint, its quirky furniture, its childish ornaments, and its bright windows reminds us how far we are from France. Nonetheless, I feel at home here, and I like it as it is. I hope that I'll settle down, and that I'll be able to work a bit. Once I know the house better, I'll talk more about it. It's been almost a week since I had a letter from home, and that's beginning to upset me. Sunday and Monday, today, which is a holiday, have brought the country to a stop. So I moved into 'Penn' on a holiday, bank holiday. It seems that this holiday was created only a dozen years ago by a very rich banker, who was so happy with his employees that he gave them a Monday off; and, slowly, this custom has been accepted across England. Now I'm told that there are three Mondays like this during the year. In any case, isn't it a good sign that I moved in on a holiday?

Tuesday, 2 August. First day in the little house. That morning, early, while the sun was on the front, I took a photograph of the house. Then I spent the morning writing these notes and reading, while Desmoulin went to the post office. Quiet day. I emptied my trunk, touched and happy at the bit of home which it contained. As I took out the small objects which I'm so familiar with and my wife was kind enough to pack, I realized how strong the links are which tie a man to the place where he lives. That's what a homeland is made of. Next, I unpacked my manuscripts and organized my work table in a small room looking out on the garden. I took an enormous amount of pleasure in doing all this; then the anxiety returned, and I wondered if I would have the strength to work. There's been such an upheaval in my life, which is normally so calm and so organized, that I'm still overwhelmed, with all my ideas in disorder. I'll have to make an enormous effort in order to get back to my writing. I have a feeling that, for a few days, I'm going to prevaricate, before starting to write my novel. Fortunately, the outline is almost finished.[25] In the evening, I finally received some letters from Paris, one in particular from my wife, which threw me into a state of uncertainty which, for me, is the worst of states. I don't know if she'll be coming to join me. Since we hadn't gone out all day, around nine o'clock we took the Oatlands road to Walton and came back by climbing up to the station and back down to our house. I wanted to buy a straw hat, among other things; but the stores were already closed and all I could find was a little bottle of 90° rubbing alcohol at the pharmacy. A gorgeous night, with a huge, bright, full moon, shining all along the beautiful, straight roads, lined with enormous trees. Park after park, with enormous lawns, deep woods, majestic silence; and the moon, in these dark woods, showering her silent silver rain over everything. Among the trees, a few bright lights shone from the windows of the houses, windows which seemed on fire. I've never had such a strong feeling of the opulence, strength, and calm of nature. I realized today that I had forgotten the umbrella which I bought in Walton the other day and my cane in the carriage which brought me here. I don't care about the umbrella, but the loss of my cane, the cane which I've taken everywhere with me for the last ten years, upset me. Just another little thing which disturbs me more than it should have, overwrought as I've been since I left France and since I've been here, alone.

Wednesday, 3 August. This morning at eleven o'clock, Desmoulin left me to return to France. The separation was less difficult than the last time, because he left me organized, safe from recognition, with my desk all ready for me to resume my work, which had been interrupted for so long. Nonetheless, when I found myself alone at lunch, I experienced a moment of real distress: far away from all that is familiar, with no one to talk to, absolutely uninformed about everything which is going on. It's odd: anxiety seems to wash over me in huge waves, with no apparent cause. After hours of calm, I'm overcome by a sense of despair, and I don't know where it comes from. I have to be reasonable: my situation isn't as bad as all that, I've got only a few dull weeks to live through. But I think that this wound inside me that won't heal comes from all the anger and all the scorn which I feel towards the abominations that are going on in France. Is this possible? Is it really me hiding here? So this is where forty years of work have led me, with a whole wretched country behind me, shouting me down and threatening me.

I spent the whole afternoon rereading my files and the notes for my novel. That did me a great deal of good. In the evening, I finalized the outline of my first chapter and promised myself that I would begin writing it tomorrow. If I don't work, if I don't get back to my daily writing schedule, I'm convinced that I'll slide into a state of deepest hypochondria. But will I be able to find myself again? Will I be able to work, obsessed as I am, weighed down by events, always waiting for new problems?[26] Desmoulin took several letters away with him; I'm waiting for replies, and this, also, feeds my uncertainty, the shivers I always feel in my nerve-wracked body when I don't know what others are going to decide. My sufferings have always come from others: my courage comes from my own will and from the decisions over which I have control.

The weather is still wonderful – a bright sun with a gusting wind which cools the air. But I didn't go out – I don't think I'll be going out a great deal.

Mme Vizetelly brought me a rented bicycle. As I went to bed, I decided to try it out tomorrow.

Thursday, 4 August. Today, at ten o'clock, I began to write my novel, *Fécondité*.[27] I worked until one o'clock and finished my usual five pages. I'm delighted with my progress and I think that if I'm left alone, I'll be able to get a great deal done here. It's been eleven months since I finished my last novel, *Paris*.[28] Almost a year of my life and my work taken from me by that monstrous affair. But I regret none of it, and I'll take up my struggle for truth and justice once again. But nonetheless, what an extraordinary adventure, at my age, after a life led entirely as a writer, a plodding, homebound writer! My only glory came through my pen and it's through my pen that I wage battle. My longstanding passion for truth has led me to a passion for justice. Oh! All those idiots and thieves! They knew nothing about me, they felt nothing, they understood nothing! So I did my usual five pages. They are simple and clear, I'm happy with them. I'm on track for another big volume; when and where will I finish it? If you'd told me, six months ago when I was writing up my initial notes, that I'd begin it in England, I'd have laughed. Now that I'm at the mercy of current events, nothing surprises me, and all I ask is the strength to continue and to finish my new work, even in the midst of the storm. My work will be, I hope, a great comfort to me. As was the case so many times in the past, my work will keep me going through the most dreadful moral upheavals.

This morning, Vizetelly sent me a few French newspapers. A wonderful article by Mirbeau, in *L'Aurore*, where he rightly says that our enemies are stuck between a public confession or a coup d'état, and that they'll choose the coup d'état.[29] That's what I've thought for a long time. Oh, what a wretched country! My heart pounds when reading a French newspaper throws me back into that terrible turmoil where the great soul of a generous and free people, the people of the French Revolution, is suffering.

This afternoon, when I decided to go for a bicycle ride to get some air, I realized that the handlebars were too narrow for my legs and hit my knees when I turned. I didn't go out. I took a bath.

Friday, 5 August. Wonderfully calm day. I didn't see anyone, I didn't go out. Shortly before ten o'clock, I got to work, and I wrote five pages of my novel. All is well. In Paris, I would have said, 'My day is complete,' no matter what happened afterwards. But here, the afternoon was very long, very difficult to endure. The sky turned grey and a high wind was blowing. I walked for only half an hour in the garden, deep in sorrow, suffering more than I would have thought from loneliness. I'm still reading *Le Rouge et le noir*, but that doesn't fill up my life. It's a very human book, nonetheless, and well constructed, which surprises me a bit: previously the structure of the book must have escaped me.[30] But reading make me unhappy, puts my nerves on edge and leaves me with a sad, empty feeling. Never one to feel bored, now I'm looking forward to the nights. What's missing is someone to love, to talk to, about others and about myself. Everyone whom I love in France seems so very far away today.

Vizetelly wrote to me this morning to tell me that, according to the English newspapers, the *Petit Journal* has been found guilty in the slander action, which I brought against it after the series of

Weybridge: The gardens of Zola's house

articles it published about my father.[31] That's fine. But there's no real punishment harsh enough for that miserable paper, which poisoned a whole nation. And the damages and fines imposed are truly a measly and hollow triumph for the legal system in the face of the numerous and devastating questions that currently face the French justice system. Oh! This is all far from over!

Saturday, 6 August. A work day. I completed my task in the morning; my mind feels extremely clear, and I'm delighted at this as I begin my novel. There'll be time enough for confusion. My mornings are a delight: I see my subject – which is an extremely complex one – clearly, and I work steadily, the way I work best. But passing the afternoons is difficult. I walked for an hour at the bottom of the little garden, near the vegetable patch, along the single path which crosses it. It's like a French garden, with squares

Oatlands Chase

of cabbages, potatoes, and peas. It makes me think of home. The only trees there are a birch and a chestnut. There are robins, very lively and cheeky, who chirp and fly about, so close you could almost touch them. They must know that I'm their friend. This amuses me for a moment, but then I think about my pets, about the naughty chevalier Pinpin, my bad-tempered little dog (whose slave I am), whom I still look for at my feet, although I've been gone now for three weeks. It's odd, these tricks of vision: it's as if he's brushed past my legs; I look for him, and I remember him.

In the afternoon, Wareham came to look at the bicycle. We took off the brakes and it will be fine; I'll just have to be careful in the turns so that the handlebars don't hit me on the knees.

Sunday, 7 August. An English Sunday, as miserable as it can be. It's pouring rain, all day the sky is slate grey, and then sprays of water rise from the ground, obscuring the horizon. I now understand the deep greens and the endless meadows in the English country-side: it is all this mild wet weather which produces all this marvel-lous growth. And from the windows of the little house, the far meadows, bordered with enormous elms and oaks, take on a vaporous lightness, like something from a fairytale. Perspectives appear, the trees in the distance are only blurred silhouettes. The clumps of trees stand out, delicately coloured. It's the haziness and the quivering of the Elysian Fields, a dream of unending gentleness and melancholy.

Vizetelly came over this morning, so I could write only three pages. He brought me some newspapers, which rekindled some of my anxieties. Our cause seems to be going well in Paris, but how many abominations still exist! Looking from here, the events strike me as acts of pure madness. Perhaps this explains the extraordinary stupor that has plagued Europe for the past six months.

As he was looking in the corner, Vizetelly found my old cane, which I had taken everywhere with me for the past ten years and I thought I had lost, which had upset me enormously. The aston-ishing thing is that it had been in the corner for six days, just across from my work table. I should have noticed it there twenty times. I think, in fact, that sometimes objects hide on us in order to test us. In spite of the rain, finding my old cane brightened the day for me.

Monday, 8 August. Today I went for my first bicycle ride. After all the rain yesterday, the roads were still a bit muddy; but they are very lovely, although I can't say that they're as good as our French roads, which are metalled, firm, and hard wearing. But in the spot where I'm living, they stretch out flat to the horizon, between beautiful parks full of lovely trees and enclosed by holly hedges so thick that even a skinny cat couldn't get through. I do admire those holly hedges: they're so thick, green, and shiny, and I think how slowly and poorly my holly hedges in Médan grow. It's truly a pleasure to cycle past these parks, these completely straight and unending hedges, between so many beautiful trees on these per-

Surrey Road

Chatham Heath

fectly straight, interminable roads. You'd think you were on the wide paths of an immense garden. What had already struck me was the number of women on bicycles. They definitely outnumber the men. And I notice that most of them aren't simply out for a ride: they are middle-class ladies, mothers, and young women who are going to the store for groceries, with their small baskets attached to the handlebars. It's perfectly clear that, because the country houses here are so far apart and so far removed from the villages, bicycles are extremely useful to the housewives, since the bicycle allows them to run all sorts of errands quickly and effortlessly. So cycling has become part of everyday household life. In France, this is still far from being the case.

And I have another confession to make. I have always decried the wearing of skirts and have always supported the wearing of divided skirts as being the only orthodox, practical and attractive alternative;[32] however, I'm deeply shaken by the sight before me of hundreds of women who pass by my window each day. English women are extremely elegant in skirts, very graceful on their bicycles, sitting up straight on the seat, with their skirts draped in long folds. What does this mean? In the Bois de Boulogne, I always found two women out of three absolutely ridiculous, horrible, looking like old ladies disguised as babies, with their huge backsides looking hilarious. Is the difference that the English women are as flat as boards and as thin as sticks? The truth is that their distinctive elegance comes from their attractive slim figures, in other words from the absence of over-voluptuous charms. In any case, I don't think I could be accused of being an ungrateful guest if I said that they look charming on their bicycles and that they've re-converted me to skirts.

I rode for an hour, through Walton and then back by another road. These little English towns are delightful, perfectly kept, and with a simple but happy appearance. I don't know where they hide poor people's houses in this country, but one certainly doesn't see them.

This morning, I made my quota, my five pages, in a good frame of mind. The first chapter is coming along.

Tuesday, 9 August. Another good morning of work. I hope to finish the first chapter tomorrow.

I didn't go out all day. It's grey and cold. It feels like November. Only towards evening the sky cleared and the sun came out for a moment. I understand why rich English people spend the winter in Cannes, Nice, Rome, or Sorrento. Yet what a wonderful countryside it is, so green, so lush, always soaked in an otherworldly mist. I never get tired of admiring it. But I get a chill nonetheless when I think that I might be forced to spend the winter here. I now better understand the expression: 'le doux pays de France.' It's unarguable that our temperate climate in Paris, with its bright sky, with both heat and cold in equal measure, has its charm. I remember coming back from Rome, how happy I was when I woke at dawn in the train as we travelled through the dew-soaked green valleys of Bourgogne. And I'm sure that when I leave here

The village of Weybridge

for France, I'll be just as glad to travel through the suburbs of Paris, touched by the sun of the last few fine days of autumn. Surrounded by all these enormous parks, I miss my friendly little garden.

Wednesday, 10 August. I finished my first chapter this morning. It's thirty-three handwritten pages long. Once again, the beginnings of a very long novel! But once again, I've chosen a huge topic, and I'll have to treat the subject with all the vastness which it implies. Also, this chapter wasn't too difficult, and I'm quite happy, although I couldn't put everything into it that I might have wanted. Now that I'm hard at work, all I have to do is carry on.

I still have no news of what's going on in France. I don't think I've read a French paper for a week. Desmoulin was supposed to have *L'Aurore* and *Le Siècle* sent to me; he even wrote that he'd

The church of Weybridge

Another view of the church of Weybridge

The Wey 1

placed the order, but I haven't received anything yet.[33] It's not that I'm desperate to know: I'm calmer and happier remaining in total ignorance. I'm still a bit disgusted by our newspapers: they've left me sick with calumny and lies, after so many months of muck-raking, as if it were pouring from a sewer. And yet at times, when I'm strolling in my little garden to stretch my legs, I suddenly raise my head, as if to listen to what's going on far away. What are they doing over there? Where are they in this abominable adventure? Are truth and justice at last coming to the fore? Will I finally be able to come home in peace, to forget this nightmare, to get back to my work as a writer? Then, all around me, I hear only the chirping of the robins flying among the cabbages, and I resign myself to wait. Perhaps it's just as well that I have no news. I know that victory is still far off.

The Wey 2

This evening the weather cleared again, after a grey day. It was very mild in the garden after dinner, and I spent a pleasant hour there.

Thursday, 11 August. I'm not going out, I'm seeing no one: what, then, could be emptier than these notes? In the morning, I get up at eight o'clock, at nine I have a cup of coffee, then I get straight to work until one o'clock. Then, after lunch, I try to kill the afternoon as best I can. In the evening, I read and go to bed at nine o'clock. The next day, I begin again. No one, nothing: it's in my poor head and my poor heart that the storm is raging, and that's a storm without end. I received some newspapers from France and I see that the French courts are still persecuting the innocent and freeing the guilty ones. They let Esterhazy go, while

The Thames, near Walton 4

Picquart, a loyal man with a clear conscience, remains behind bars. A country where this sort of abomination is permitted is a country which has fallen to the lowest levels of shame. There's no longer the smallest iota of protection for brave and equitable people. I've made up my mind: I shall not return until justice has been re-established in France.

This morning, I began my second chapter. It's only when I'm writing that I feel calm, happy.

Friday, 12 August. Another day just like yesterday: it seems that is all I have to write each night, unless they pursue me further. I'm certain that I must have been recognized at the hotel where I stayed for ten days. There was a note in one of the papers, saying that I was staying there under the name 'Beauchamp,' with a

The Thames, near Walton 5

friend called Valentin.[34] Now if this note becomes widely known and if curious people begin to look for me, it won't be difficult for them to find me here. I'm so tired and so irritated that I think that I might just do nothing. My whole being protests furiously against this ferocious, idiotic persecution, which results purely and simply from my love of truth and justice. I think that if anything more happens, I'm going to throw all my feelings of revolt and indignation right in the face of that country which has been so unjust towards me – me, who has done nothing but love my country. I'm fed up – I've done my duty, I only want one thing – to get back to work in peace and quiet. If I have to, I'll live here – I'll live somewhere else – in any quiet corner of the world, and I'll continue to work. This will be another way to love and

Virginia Water

serve a country which is now dishonoured by a gang of despicable wrongdoers, whose names will go down in history.

Saturday, 13 August. The weather has turned fine again; it's stifling, and I'm suffering in the small room with lots of glass where I'm working, since the sun's turning it into a hothouse. But the same peace, the same solitude. It seems that the Court of Appeal has doubled the fine in the action which the handwriting experts began against me.[35] That's going to cost me about 40,000 francs. Oh, let them take it all, let them sell all my belongings, so that I own nothing whatsoever in France. They think I'm rich, when, in fact, I don't even have 100,000 francs coming in. When I'm financially ruined and when they see me in exile, in some far

W. Harriss, boatbuilder

corner writing for a living, perhaps then they'll have the grace to keep silent. As long as I have my health, as long as I can hold a pen, I'll be able to survive. I began life poor; poverty may return; I'm not afraid of it. I'll never be happier than the day when they leave me alone, when I can write in peace what I feel I must write. The greatest good, the greatest happiness, is to be able to write with freedom.

I was bored today. I finished *Le Rouge et le noir.* The love affair between Julien and Mme de Rênal is extremely touching; but his affair with Mathilde de La Mole is the most complicated and difficult thing I can imagine. At least I see things so differently that this sort of story, narrated at such great length, exasperates me. Stendhal's world of nobles also bothers me a great deal. I'd like to have had the time to write a study on him, and I think I'd

The church in Virginia Water

The church in Virginia Water, another view

The church of Wisley

The church of Wisley, another view

Zola's house in Addlestone

have some interesting things to say, simply because we have opposite views on questions of emotion and feeling.[36]

Sunday, 14 August, to Tuesday, 23 August. I've stopped making my
notes each day, because my days are all the same. I always work in
the morning, sometimes I go out for a bicycle ride in the afternoon. I go to Walton or to Weybridge, the two little villages
between which my house is situated. I've taken photographs of
these two towns, of the banks of the Wey and of the Thames.
Again, the countryside is charming, with beautiful roads lined
with large parks and huge trees. When I go into a store, I get what
I want by pointing to it, and, in order to pay, I've learned to count
in English, so that I can manage.
    I'd noticed at the hotel, and I notice every day how discreet the

Summerfield's grounds, Addlestone

English are, the complete liberty which they demand for themselves and they respect in others. On the street, in the villages,
everyone knows that I'm French, because I do feel different when
I go out on my bicycle. And yet no one seems surprised, no one
makes fun of me. They don't seem to notice me; they don't
bother me. In the stores, when I can't make myself understood,
they smile, but in a kind way, and we always end up understanding
each other. The other day, the chain on my bicycle became loose.
It felt as if the wheel were malfunctioning. Since I didn't have the
tools I needed with me, I went to a bicycle repair shop in Weybridge.
I had to wait for a workman, and it wasn't easy making myself
understood or understanding. Finally, he grasped what I wanted,
and he carried out the minor repair very adeptly. Other than that,

Spinney Hill, Addlestone (Zola's garden wall on the right)

my rides have been uneventful, very calm and always the same. I
go out only in order to get a bit of exercise.

During the long days I spend in this little house, I amuse myself
by studying and noting the differences between English and French
country houses. I'm talking about the middle-class houses and
shops, which exist in abundance in the outskirts of London. What
strikes me most of all is the need to crowd together, one house
right beside the other. For the poorer houses too, the houses of
the suburban workers, this swarming together is typical, with all
the units absolutely identical. Entire streets, whole districts are
made up of these identical little houses, glued one to another. It's
like a phalanstery come to life – the dreams of our communist
thinkers come true. In France, these workers' cities have never

The village of Addlestone

succeeded. Building affordable houses for our workers in France has been tried a number of times, but all the attempts have ended in failure. The only things I've seen which resemble these English workers' houses are the miners' lodgings in the north of France; and there, the workers grumble, saying that they are penned up like animals. In the outskirts of Paris, there would be a general uprising – the workers would protest that they were being imprisoned, that they were being forced to live in barracks. The uniformity would strike them as a sort of control, a yoke which would prevent them from expressing any imagination, any individuality. They'd rather be less well housed than be housed exactly like their neighbours. Which leads one to suppose that there is, in the English working class, a more practical and more informed view of communism, or at least of its benefits. But what invalidates this

Another view of the village of Addlestone

explanation, at least up to a point, is that we're told that nowhere else is individualism more strongly felt or more widely practised than in England. But I keep coming back to the little English house, replicating itself by the millions in the great parks of the past, which are now divided into small lots. The high price of land is undoubtedly a factor in the dense groupings of these houses. But there's also the need to stick together, about which I was talking. As soon as one house goes up in a vacant lot, you can be sure that others will spring up right beside it. They appear to be built very cheaply, out of bricks and plaster. The walls are like cardboard, and this is why, during the few short weeks of hot sun, it's like being roasted on a spit. All the more so, since, because of the great number of large windows and the absolute lack of shutters and blinds, they turn into hothouses. In addition, despite

Addlestone Station

all those glass panes, only a few of them actually open, which leads
to a lack of ventilation. One boils – and I don't know if in the
winter the fireplaces produce sufficient heat. Moreover, I've noticed that the rooms very rarely open one into the other; they all
open onto the hall or onto a large, practical landing. Generally,
there's no separate toilet; each bedroom has a toilet in the corner,
and in each room there is a cheval glass on the table. I find this to
be a fault in the English system, since the addition of even the
smallest washroom would free up the bedroom, and make it
healthier and cleaner. The lavatories and the bathrooms are well
arranged. They're all connected to the main drainage and in
almost all the new houses there are water heaters which provide
hot water for the kitchen, the bathtub, and the sink. There are

Addlestone's fields

other details, too, which I like – the solid thickness of the doors, beautifully built; the excellent quality of the door hardware, keys made as small as possible, bolts which fit into the strike plate exactly, strong bolts, beautifully finished. All the rooms in the little house where I live are painted in light colours – soft green, soft rose, soft yellow; the woodwork, as a contrast, stands out against these pale colours – peacock green, bright brown, dark orange. It's very pleasant to look at. There are rugs everywhere, the staircase, with its pine bannister, is carpeted. But with the exception of a few old pieces of furniture in mahogany, the rest of the furniture is disgraceful. The ornaments, especially, are enough to bring tears to one's eyes. It's childish and ugly. I've never seen such bad taste. There are some English engravings, technically

Another view of Addlestone's fields

well executed, but whose subjects are simply extraordinary. The animals in them play an overly sentimental role. I like dogs a great deal, but it bothers me when they echo the melancholy of their young mistresses, exchanging soulful looks with them. They overdo the use of dogs – a dog with a child, a dog with a grandfather, a dog with a beggarwoman. Then horses – horses also echoing all sorts of human feelings, made so human that they are capable of expressing the most complex human dramas. On the wall in front of me, there's a picture of three horses' heads at the drinking trough, almost life-sized, which has haunted me since I arrived. Then there are squirrels nibbling hazelnuts, sparrows fluttering about in the snow, butterflies on roses. All in all, it's just sentimentality, and I do believe that these people have kind hearts.

'The Castle,' Oatlands Chase, Surrey (the original of the haunted house in Zola's story *Angéline*)

Another view of 'The Castle,' Oatlands Chase, Surrey

I confess that I'm having more difficulty getting used to the cooking. It's true that my cook is a good lady who has cooked only for families of modest means. But that shows me at least how these families eat. Never any salt in anything. All the vegetables boiled and served without butter or oil. The large roasts of meat are good, but the braised cutlets and steaks are uneatable. And I'm so wary of the sauces that I've banned them absolutely. And the bread – good God, English bread, barely cooked, all soft, like a sponge. They eat hardly any bread here. Nonetheless, I'm living perfectly well on roasted meat, ham, eggs, and salad. And I'm not talking about cooking just to complain, but to express my astonishment – philosophically – at the gulf there is between a French pot au feu and English oxtail soup. We may at some

Another view of 'The Castle,' Oatlands Chase, Surrey

A view of the village of Norwood

point bring the two nations' people to embrace one another, but we'll never be able to bring them together on the question of cooking. Even when we're all brothers, we'll still fight over the question of whether potatoes should be served with or without butter.

Tuesday, 23 August, to Friday, 21 October. I've stopped making notes for a long while now, but I wanted to make note of at least a few dates. I left 'Penn' on Saturday, 27 August and went to 'Summerfield.' I stayed there six weeks, until 10 October. I went next to London, until Saturday the 15th, when I came to Upper Norwood.

During that time, I heard about all the repercussions of what was happening in Paris; I'd only have to organize them by date in

Another view of the village of Norwood

order to chart my days of hope and of despair. I lost my poor Pinpin, who died on Tuesday, 20 September. I found out about it only on Wednesday the 28th. The enormous sorrow that I felt. From Friday the 23rd, I was obliged to set my novel aside, and I didn't get back to it until Thursday, 20 October, at Upper Norwood. I spent the three days before that Thursday writing my novella, *Angéline.*

Charpentier arrived at 'Summerfield' on Tuesday, 1 October, and didn't leave London until Wednesday the 12th. And those are, more or less, the important dates.

I must describe 'Summerfield,' the large garden, half-wild, with a huge pit, no doubt a former sandpit, which someone had turned into a flowerbed. The tennis court, the wicker lawn chair where I spent so many hours each morning struggling with the

Church in the village of Norwood

A street of Norwood with The Crystal Palace in the background

Daily Telegraph or the *Standard*, at first not understanding a word of English, trying, with the help of the dictionary, to read the bulletins from France, then, finally, getting the gist of them. It was after I received Larat's telegram – 'Tell Beauchamp immediately about the victory' – that I went to buy the two papers for the first time; and my angst, faced with this strange language, with these sentences, which were so vitally interesting to me but remained unfathomable, my desperate effort, my struggle, to understand them, to know what was happening. Describe this. And the same thing happened each morning for weeks. The English grammar book which I read, not in order to learn the language, but in order to understand what it is. What I think about the English language.

There could certainly be an interesting psychological study

The Crystal Palace, a view from afar

done on the moods I went through as reports on the affair arrived. First of all, the moment of absolute joy, after Henry's confession, around 1 September (check the date). I thought that the affair was over, that a review would take place, amid cries of anger, cries for justice. Then, my feelings as new complications arose, as new obstacles surfaced. What! All of France was not rising up, truth was not dawning on everyone? Then, the despair into which I slowly sank, the absolute pessimism. Although I was calm during my own trial, I'd now lost faith, I felt that France was lost. I spent terrible weeks, in despair over a country where justice seemed completely dead. The tragedy and the horror, the echoes in me of the terrible things happening in my country, these echoes in my solitude, in this strange and inimical country, where I didn't have a living soul to speak to. This emptiness, this loss of

The Crystal Palace, a closer view

grace lasted until the day when the Supreme Court of Appeal was convened; and even then, I continued to live in fear of trickery, always dreading some supreme infamy which would bury the crime forever. I've now got to the point of wondering – now that I'm almost sure that truth will triumph – whether France will ever acknowledge those who saved her from shame. The underlying causes, which blinded her for so long – royalist and military atavism, the incurable cancer of defeat, the unsatisfied pride of the legendary French soldier, the master of the world – these causes won't disappear overnight; they continue to prevail, to such an extent that many people won't thank us for having reconciled France with her ideals of humanity and justice. They're still fixed on the image of the French flag flying over all of Europe; the future is closed for them.[37] Is it not enough for them to be a

Upper Norwood

generous and just nation? Would they rather remain in the present
than hear a cry of deliverance from the entire country? We'll have
to wait for history to judge us, once all the deplorable political
and social conditions of today have disappeared.

In my notes, I must remember, too, my day-to-day life at
'Summerfield,' my walks to Chertsey, Chobham, Byfleet, Shepper-
ton, Windsor. The accident, the man who broke his leg in front
of my house, the man all alone on the road, in the shadows, the
lady who gave him first aid by the light of a lantern, and the
policeman who helped him up and bandaged his leg so effi-
ciently, and the short speech of thanks he made to the lady.[38] At
that same moment, in France, the police were beating people.
The crows, their massed departure each evening into the huge
fields across from me.

A view of the Queen's Hotel gardens

The maids, the shopkeepers, the cooking, the mores, the habits.

The beautiful weather, days spent in the garden under a bright, sunny sky.

The room where I worked, which had only one, heavy door, sliding in the grooves it had made; the terrible noise, the rumbling of the door, when one opened or closed it; the solitude of the room, as if I were shut away, at the bottom of a dungeon, over which someone had pushed a slab, forever.

The sad days I spent in the little living room, in front of the first coal fires of the season, after the death of my poor Pinpin.

The photographs I took everywhere.

Divide all these things over the time period, taking the dates into careful account and putting the facts back into chronological

Another view of the Queen's Hotel gardens

order; my arrival at 'Summerfield,' move to the short stay in London, then my arrival here, in Norwood; then my moving in, my first walks, one or two hours a day, the hilly countryside, the steep drops, the extraordinary views of the Crystal Palace. Describe the Queen's Hotel. My two rooms overlooking the garden, with the cottages on the horizon. The waiter who serves me and doesn't speak French; and entire days of silence. I read, I write, I'm never bored.

Notes

1 Zola's writings from England were first published in French by
Professor Colin Burns ('Émile Zola: *Pages d'exil.*')
2 See the introduction.
3 Jane Charpentier was the daughter of Georges Charpentier, Zola's
publisher and close friend.
4 Zola's expression in the original text is 'en candélabre,' a difficult
phrase to translate, but one which means that the police officers
were standing on guard.
5 From 20 September to 1 October 1893 Zola was the guest of the
English Institute of Journalists. Their annual conference was a great
success, extensively covered by the British and French press. Zola
was celebrated as a journalist, as the author of the *Rougon-Macquart*,
as well as the 'incarnation' of France's intellectual and cultural
glory. The various events of this visit are narrated in the very detailed study by Burns ('Le voyage de Zola à Londres en 1893.')
See also Zola, *Correspondance*, vol. VII, 36–7; henceforth cited *CZ.*
6 The Grosvenor Hotel was right next to Victoria Station. Vizetelly
recounts the incident that marked Zola's arrival in London: 'There
was, however, one thing that [Zola] did not know, and that was the
close proximity of this hotel to the railway station. So, having secured
a hansom, he briefly told the Jehu to drive him to the Grosvenor.
At this, cabby looked down from his perch in sheer astonishment.
Then, doubtless, in a considerate and honest spirit – for there are
still some considerate and honest cabbies in London – he tried to
explain matters. At all events he spoke at length. But M. Zola failed

to understand him. 'Grosvenor Hotel,' repeated the novelist; and then, seeing that cabby seemed bent on further expostulation, he resolutely took his seat in the vehicle. ... However, cabby said no more, or if he did his words failed to reach M. Zola. The reins were jerked, the scraggy night-horse broke into a spasmodic trot, turned out of the station, and pulled up in front of the caravansary ... Zola was astonished at reaching his destination with such despatch, and suddenly became conscious of cabby's real motive in expostulating with him' (Vizetelly, *With Zola in England*, p. 11–12).

7 Zola, his friends and allies decided to use pseudonyms when corresponding, in an attempt to fool the French police. For example, Zola was, in turn, 'Monsieur Pascal,' 'Emile Beauchamp,' 'M. Roger,' and 'Jean Richard.' Moreover, letters were never sent directly to Zola's address, but rather to a third party (usually to the solicitor F.W. Wareham).

8 The reader will remember that upon arriving in London, Zola wrote immediately to Ernest Vizetelly. See Introduction, p. 7.

9 Bernard-Lazare (1865–1903) was a poet and a literary critic. In 1895 he met with Mathieu Dreyfus, Alfred's brother, and soon became convinced of the captain's innocence. Bernard-Lazare published several articles in *L'Aurore* in favour of Alfred Dreyfus.

10 *L'Aurore* (1 October 1897–2 August 1914) was a left-wing, Republican daily, founded by Georges Clemenceau. 'J'Accuse,' Zola's famous article on the Affair, was published on the front page on 18 January 1898. *L'Aurore* also published Zola's *Fécondité* (*Fruitfulness*, the novel written during the exile in England), from 15 May to 4 October 1899.

11 After the fall of the house of Vizetelly & Co., Andrew Chatto and his partner, Percy Spalding, became the 'official' publishers of Zola in England, starting with *The Downfall* in 1893, in Ernest Vizetelly's translation. The incident mentioned by Zola is recounted by Vizetelly, who believed the two ladies were French actresses. The day after the alarming encounter, Vizetelly visited MM. Chatto and Spalding: 'When Mr Spalding made his appearance he greeted me with a smile, and while leading the way to his private room exclaimed, "So our friend Zola is in London!" "How do you know that?" "Why, my wife saw him yesterday in Buckingham Palace Road"' (Vizetelly, *With Zola in England*, 33–4).

12 During the last two weeks of July newspapers published several unfounded reports about Zola's whereabouts: some claimed that the writer had been seen in Sweden, others in Belgium, the Netherlands, Norway, or Switzerland. Zola was also caricatured having tea with the emperor of China or kissing the Pope's ring.

13 *Le Rouge et le noir* (1830) and *La Chartreuse de Parme* (1839) by Stendhal (1783–1842) were certainly two of the most famous and celebrated novels of the nineteenth century and had been commented upon by Zola. See notes 17 and 24.

14 In 1878 Zola had bought a country house in the village of Médan, outside Paris, where he spent six months a year with his wife, writing and playing host to his friends. A book was to come out of these friendly meetings with Maupassant, Paul Alexis, Henry Céard, Léon Hennique, and J.-K. Huysmans: *Les Soirées de Médan* (1880). Verneuil was the country house where Jeanne Rozerot and the children used to spend the summer. Anti-Semitic newspapers were indiscreetly scrutinizing both houses and publishing reports about Zola's wife and his mistress.

15 According to Colin Burns, on 25 July 1898 the *Daily Chronicle* had mentioned Zola's presence in London. Reporters had embroidered the report, however, with details which were untrue, stating, for example, that Madame Zola was also in London. See Zola, *Oeuvres complètes*, vol. 14, 1171 (henceforth cited *OC*).

16 Like Zola, Fabrice del Dongo, protagonist of *La Chartreuse de Parme*, finds himself at one point in the novel spending his days in solitude, a prisoner.

17 In an early analysis of Stendhal, which was first published as a series of articles in 1880–1, Zola maintained that he preferred *Le Rouge et le noir* to *La Chartreuse de Parme*. In the first place, he found the characters of *La Chartreuse de Parme* more typical of the Italy of the fifteenth century than of the present. Further, he was critical of Stendhal's literary style and structure: 'The novel has no centre; it moves from episode to episode. After an interminable introduction, the novel finishes abruptly, just as the author has begun a new plot line' (*Les Romanciers naturalistes, OC*, vol. 10, 92).

18 On 2 August Zola wrote to Eugène Fasquelle, thanking him for sending the money and promising to send a receipt as soon as possible. 'Please don't be annoyed with me,' he added, 'if you don't

hear from me for a while. It's better that I disappear for another few weeks. However I keep my memories of my friends in my heart. I think about them, and I'm very touched to know that they're thinking about me' (*CZ*, vol. X, letter 161).

19 The French text mentions 'fenêtres libres,' probably referring to the fact that French windows open wide, like doors.

20 The French texts reads, 'une sorte de mauvais lieu,' which could refer to a brothel.

21 Alexandrine had sent a large trunk from Paris, with the preparatory notes for the novel *Fécondité* (which Zola was to write in England; see note 25), various personal belongings, and Zola's photographic equipment.

22 Wareham and Vizetelly were very wary of any stranger asking for Zola, for fear of having the Versailles judgment served on the novelist. According to Vizetelly, Wareham 'had received a visit from a most singular-looking little Frenchman, who had presented one of Maître Labori's visiting cards and requested an interview with M. Zola. Questioned as to his business, the only explanation he would give was that he had with him a document in a sealed envelope which he must place in M. Zola's own hands.' A careful cross-examination revealed that the envoy was carrying 'a long letter from Maître Labori, accompanied by a document concerning the prosecution which had been instituted with reference to the infamous articles' published by the *Petit Journal* concerning Zola's father (Vizetelly, *With Zola in England*, 93–100).

23 These two articles, by Jacques Dhur, appeared in *La Petite République française* on 28 July and 30 July 1898.

24 *Le Rouge et le noir*, Stendhal's second novel, first appeared in 1830. Based on a true story, *Le Rouge et le noir* recounts the social ascent of a young man, Julien Sorel, and his death by execution as a result of his attempted murder of Mme de Rênal, a former mistress.

25 Zola had begun the planning and the research for *Fécondité* in December of the previous year. When he left Paris on 18 July 1898, he had already virtually completed his outline. Zola began to write the novel itself on 4 August.

26 From his earliest years, Zola had always considered work not only as an important intellectual discipline, but as a means of overcoming

difficulty and grief. When his beloved mother died in 1880, Zola
wrote to Marguerite Charpentier, the wife of his publisher, 'I'm
going to try to lose myself in my work' (*CZ*, vol. IV, letter 48).

27 On Zola's highly structured work habits, see the Introduction.

28 Zola finished writing his novel on 31 August 1897. The last install-
ment of *Paris* appeared in *Le Journal* on 9 February 1898 and in
volume form, published by Charpentier, on 1 March 1898.

29 Octave Mirbeau, critic and novelist, published his denunciation
in *L'Aurore* on 2 August 1898. In his article, Mirbeau outlined the
dilemma which faced their common enemies: 'Public confession
of a crime implies nobility, heroism, greatness of soul. So they will
strike out. That's easier, and it's more in line with their sort of
moral beauty ... Murder is in the air. For a week now, they've been
harping on about assassination in the name of our country, exalting
it and glorifying it in God's name.'

30 Zola was an admirer of Stendhal, seeing in him a precursor of the
Naturalist movement; in his critical writings, however, Zola had
found Stendhal's plots contrived and his characters incomplete:
'Stendhal has taken a man's head, in order to carry out psychological experiments. Balzac has taken the entire man, with his organs,
his natural and social environment, and supplemented the psychol-
ogist's experiments with the experiments of the physiologist' (*Les
Romanciers naturalistes, OC*, vol. 11, 94).

31 In May 1898 Ernest Judet, editor of the anti-Semitic newspaper *Le
Petit Journal*, had published two articles in which he attacked Zola's
father, accusing François Zola of stealing money from the French
army when he was an officer in 1831. In all, Judet published four
articles, tarring father and son with the same brush. Zola sued Judet
for slander, and won.

32 Zola was interviewed in the press on several occasions about his
enthusiasm for cycling and in 1893 had been named an honorary
member of the Touring Club de France. In the novel *Paris*, Zola's
opinion on appropriate cycling dress for women is voiced by Marie,
future wife of the novel's protagonist: 'But can you understand it?
To think that women have an unique opportunity of putting themselves at their ease, and releasing their limbs from prison, and yet
they won't do so! If they think that they look the prettier in short

skirts like schoolgirls they are vastly mistaken! And as for any question of modesty, well it seems to me that it is infinitely less objec-
tionable for women to wear rationals than to bare their bosoms at
balls and theatres and dinners as society ladies do' (*Paris*, trans. E.A.
Vizetelly [London: Chatto & Windus, 1898], 333–4). The 'rationals'
of which Vizetelly speaks are divided skirts, a popular garment for
female cyclists in France at the turn of the century.

33 On 12 August, still without his newspapers, Zola wrote to Desmoulin: 'You know that I'm still not getting *L'Aurore* or *Le Siècle*.
I'd appreciate it if you could do *everything possible* so that they don't
forget about me. This complete lack of French newspapers is really
getting on my nerves' (*CZ*, vol. X, letter 172).

34 'Valentin' was the pseudonym chosen for Fernand Desmoulin.

35 The English newspapers had reported on 11 August that the Court
of Appeal had handed down its decision on the 10 August, award-
ing 10,000 francs to each of the experts, instead of the 5,000 francs
originally stipulated. The sum of 2,000 francs, representing a fine
levied on Zola himself, was not modified.

36 Zola had presented his 1881 analysis of Stendhal's *Le Rouge et le noir*
and *La Chartreuse de Parme* not as a complete study, but as a series
of reflections based on a reading of the novels, 'pencil in hand.'
Stendhal's lack of emotion and feeling represented one of Zola's
chief criticisms of the works in question: 'Stendhal's characters are
intellectual speculations rather than living beings' (*Les Romanciers
naturalistes*, *OC*, vol. 10, 94).

37 The sentence which follows offers something of a syntactic and
grammatical puzzle. Whether it represents an error on Zola's part
or a faulty transcription of the original manuscript is impossible
to determine. As presented in the *Oeuvres complètes*, the sentence
reads: 'De là le malaise de n'être qu'un peuple généreux et juste,
au lieu du cri de délivrance que devrait pousser la nation entière'
(*OC*, vol. 14, 1160).

38 According to Zola's daughter, the lady in question was Jeanne
Rozerot, who visited the novelist in England on two occasions,
accompanied by their two children. See Denise Le Blond-Zola,
Émile Zola raconté par sa fille (Paris: Fasquelle, 1931), 262.

Select Bibliography

Bryois, Henri. 'Les trois derniers livres des *Rougon-Macquart*,' *Le Figaro*, 2 April 1890.

Burns, Colin. 'Émile Zola: *Pages d'exil*, publiées et annotées par Colin Burns,' *Nottingham French Studies* 3: 1–2 (May–October 1964), 2–46; 48–62.

– 'Le voyage de Zola à Londres en 1893.' *Les Cahiers naturalistes* 60 (1986), 41–73.

– 'Le retentissement de l'Affaire Dreyfus dans la presse britannique en 1898–1899; esquisse d'un projet de recherches futures,' *Les Cahiers naturalistes* 54 (1980), 251–7.

Cohenoff, Alfred. 'Zola et la photographie: amateur, reporter ou artiste?' *Les Cahiers naturalistes* 66 (1992), 285–301.

Guillemot, Maurice. *Villégiatures d'artistes*. Paris: Flammarion, 1897.

Kleeblatt, Norman L., ed. *The Dreyfus Affair: Art, Truth and Justice*. Berkeley: University of California Press, 1987.

LeRoy, Edmond. 'À propos d'un nouveau roman,' *Le Journal*, 27 October 1897.

Massin, 'Émile Zola: la passion de la photographie,' *Les Cahiers naturalistes* 66 (1992), 237–41.

Norwood Society. *Émile Zola: Photographer in Norwood, South London, 1898–1899*. London: Norwood Society, 1997.

Pagès, Alain, ed. *Émile Zola: The Dreyfus Affair. 'J'Accuse' and Other Writings*. New Haven, Conn.: Yale University Press, 1996.

Speirs, D.E. and Y. Portebois, 'Emile Zola in the *Westminster Gazette*,' *Bulletin of the Émile Zola Society* (April 2001), 7–14.

– eds. *'Mon cher Maître': Lettres d'Ernest Vizetelly à Émile Zola, 1891–1902*. Montreal: Presses de l'Université de Montréal, 2002.

Spont, Henry. 'L'évolution sociale et la jeunesse: M. Émile Zola,' *Gil Blas*, 12 May 1893.

Vizetelly, Ernest. *Émile Zola: Novelist and Reformer*. London: John Lane The Bodley Head, 1904.

– *With Zola in England*. London: Chatto & Windus, 1899.

Wilson, Nelly. 'Zola and the Dreyfus Affair,' *Bulletin of the Émile Zola Society* 3 (1991), 3–9.

Zola, Émile. *Correspondance*. Ed. B.H. Bakker. Montreal/Paris: Presses de l'Université de Montréal/CNRS, 1975–95.

– 'Pages d'exil.' Ed. Colin Burns. In *Oeuvres complètes*, Vol. 14, 1125–80. Paris: Cercle du Livre précieux, 1964.

Index